VOLUME 7

THE AGE OF REVOLUTION

THE ILLUSTRATED
HISTORY OF THE WORLD

VOLUME 7

THE AGE OF
REVOLUTION

J. M. ROBERTS

New York
Oxford University Press

The Illustrated History of the World

This edition first published in 1999 in the United States of America by
Oxford University Press, Inc.,
198 Madison Avenue, New York, N.Y. 10016
Oxford is a registered trademark of Oxford University Press

THE AGE OF REVOLUTION
Copyright © Editorial Debate SA 1998
Text Copyright © J. M. Roberts 1976, 1980, 1983, 1987, 1988, 1992, 1998
Artwork and Diagrams Copyright © Editorial Debate SA 1998
(for copyright of photographs and maps, see acknowledgments on pages 191–92, which
are to be regarded as an extension of this copyright)

Art Direction by Duncan Baird Publishers
Produced by Duncan Baird Publishers, London, England
and Editorial Debate, Madrid, Spain

Series ISBN 0-19-521529-X
Volume ISBN 0-19-521525-7

DBP staff:
Senior editor: Joanne Levêque
Assistant editors: Georgina Harris, Kirsty Seymour-Ure
Senior designer: Steven Painter
Assistant designer: Anita Schnable
Picture research: Julia Ruxton
Sales fulfilment: Ian Smalley
Map artwork: Russell Bell
Decorative borders: Lorraine Harrison

Editorial Debate staff:
Editors and picture researchers:
Isabel Belmonte Martínez, Feliciano Novoa Portela,
Ruth Betegón Díez, Dolores Redondo
Editorial coordination: Ana Lucía Vila

Typeset in Sabon 11/15 pt
Colour reproduction by Trescan, Madrid, Spain
Printed in Singapore by Imago Limited

NOTE
The abbreviations CE and BCE are used throughout this book:
CE Common Era (the equivalent of AD)
BCE Before Common Era (the equivalent of BC)

10 9 8 7 6 5 4 3 2

CONTENTS

THE AGE OF REVOLUTION

Between 1500 and 1800, significant changes took place in the way educated Europeans saw their society. Important scientific discoveries were made and the Enlightenment brought a new sense of responsibility and reason. In spite of such changes, however, in the middle of the eighteenth century most people in the world (and perhaps most Europeans, too) could still believe that history would go on much as it seemed always to have done. The weight of the past was everywhere enormous and often it was immovable: some of the European efforts to shake it off have been touched upon, but nowhere outside Europe was even the possibility of doing so grasped. Though in many parts of the world a few people's lives had begun to be revolutionized by contact with Europeans, most of it was unaffected and much of it was untouched by such contamination of traditional ways.

In the next century and a half change was to come thick and fast almost everywhere and to ignore the fact was to be much harder if not impossible. By 1900 it was obvious that in Europe and the European world of settlement change had irreversibly cut off much of the traditional past. Just as important, impulses from northern Europe and the Atlantic world have also radiated outwards to transform both Europe's relations with the rest of the world and the very foundations of their lives for many of its peoples, however much some of them regretted and resisted it. By the end of the nineteenth century (and this is only an approximate and convenient marker) a world once regulated by tradition was on a new course. Its destiny was now to be continuing and accelerating transformation and the second adjective was as important as the first. A man born in 1800 who lived out the psalmist's span of three-score years and ten could have seen the world more changed in his lifetime than it had been in the previous thousand years.

The consolidation of the European world hegemony was central to these changes and one of the great motors propelling them. By 1900 European civilization had shown itself to be the most successful which had ever existed. People might not always agree on what was most important about it but no one could deny that it had produced wealth on an unprecedented scale and that it dominated the rest of the globe by power and influence as no previous civilization had ever done. Europeans (or their descendants) ran the world. Much of their domination was political, a matter of direct rule. Large areas of the world had been peopled by European stocks. As for the non-European countries still formally and politically independent of Europe, most of them had in practice to defer to European wishes and accept European interference in their affairs. Few indigenous peoples could resist, and if they did Europe often won its subtlest victory of all, for successful resistance required the adoption of European practices and, therefore, Europeanization in another form.

Leonardo da Vinci (1452–1519), whose *Diagram of the proportions of the body* is seen here, was an accomplished architect, sculptor, painter, writer, engineer, scientist and inventor – the definitive all-round "Renaissance man". The ideas of the Renaissance and its spirit of enquiry were profoundly influential on Europe's development.

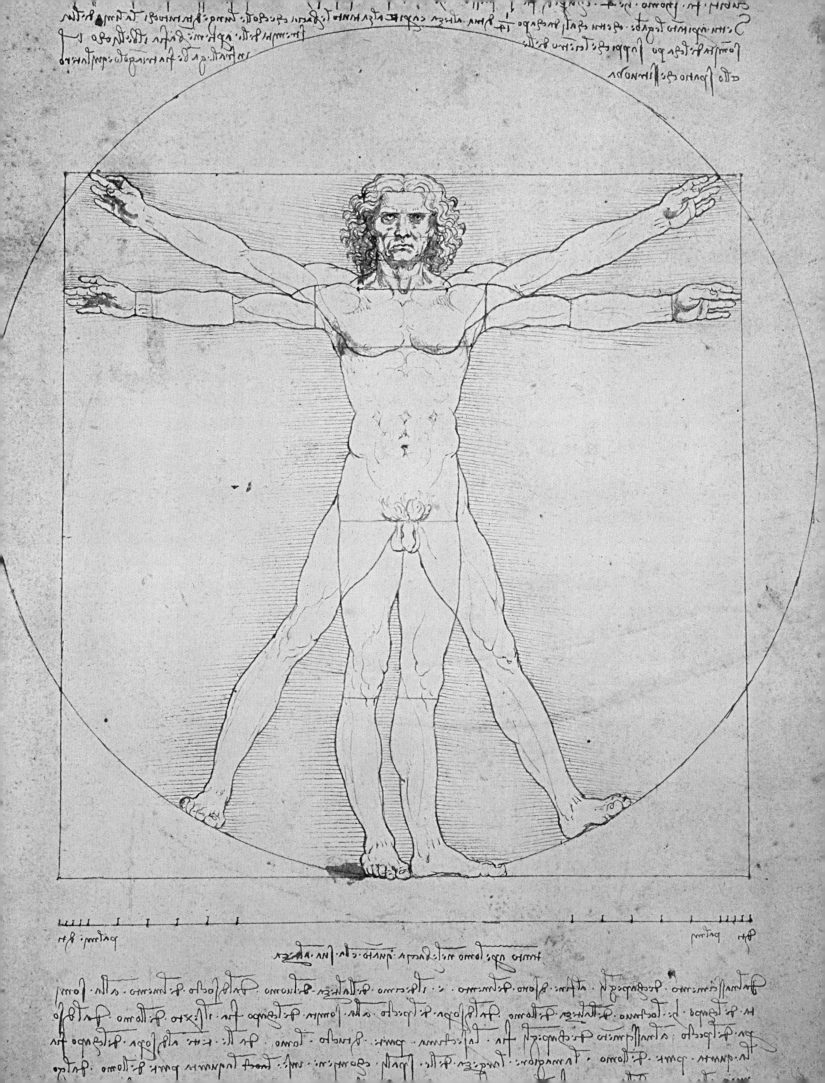

1 IDEAS OLD AND NEW

THE ESSENCE OF THE CIVILIZATION Europe was exporting to the rest of the globe between 1500 and 1800 lay in ideas. The limits they imposed and the possibilities they offered shaped the way in which that civilization operated. What is more, although the twentieth century has done great damage to them, the leading ideas adumbrated by Europeans during that period still provide most of the guide-posts by which we make our way. European culture was then given a secular foundation; it was then, too, that there took hold a progressive notion of historical development as movement towards an apex at which Europeans felt themselves to stand. Finally it was then that there grew up a confidence that scientific knowledge used in accordance with utilitarian criteria would make possible limitless progress. In short, the civilization of the Middle Ages at last came to an end in the minds of thinking men and women.

THE WEIGHT OF THE PAST

Things rarely happen cleanly and neatly in history, and only a few Europeans would have been aware of any change in popular consciousness by 1800. The traditional institutions of monarchy, hereditary status, society and religion still held sway over most of the continent in that year. Only a hundred years before there had been no civil marriage anywhere in Europe and there was still none over most of it. Barely twenty years before 1800 the last heretic had been burned in Poland and even in England an eighteenth-century monarch had, like medieval kings, touched for the king's evil (scrofula). The seventeenth century, indeed, had in one or two respects even shown regression. In both Europe and North America there was an epidemic of witch-hunting far more widespread than anything in the Middle Ages (Charlemagne had condemned witch-burners to death and canon law had forbidden belief in the night flights and other supposed pranks of witches as pagan). Nor was this the end of superstition. The last English wizard was harried to his death by his neighbours well after 1700 and a Protestant Swiss was legally executed by his countrymen for witchcraft in 1782. The Neapolitan cult of St Januarius was still of political importance in the era of the French Revolution because the successful

Known as the "Tempietto", this colonnade in the courtyard of St Peter's Church in Monteno, Rome, was commissioned by Ferdinand and Isabella of Spain and built c.1502 by Donato Bramante (c.1444–1514). During the Renaissance and Enlightenment periods, the Roman Catholic Church – the only Christian Church to have its own territorial state – consciously presented itself as a solid, monumental institution and this was reflected in its architecture.

This view of St Peter's in Rome was painted by the Dutch artist Gaspar van Wittel (1653–1736).

or unsuccessful liquefaction of the saint's blood was believed to indicate divine pleasure or displeasure at what the government was doing. Penology was still barbarous; some crimes were thought so atrocious as to merit punishment of exceptional ferocity and it was as parricides that the assassin of Henry IV of France and the attempted assassin of Louis XV suffered their abominable torments. The second died under them in 1757, only a few years before the publication of the most influential advocacy of penal reform that has ever been written. The glitter of modernity in the eighteenth century can easily deceive us;

in societies which produced art of exquisite refinement and outstanding examples of chivalry and honour, popular amusements focused on the pleasures of bear-baiting, cock-fighting or pulling the heads off geese.

ORGANIZED RELIGION

The culture of the people is often an aspect of society which shows most obviously the weight of the past, but until almost the end of these three centuries much of the formal and institutional apparatus which upheld the past

Many Europeans long remained fascinated with super-stition, fortune-telling and witchcraft. This Spanish painting, *The Witches' Coven*, was painted by Francisco de Goya in 1821–1822.

also remained intact over most of Europe. The most striking example to modern eyes would be the primacy still enjoyed almost everywhere in the eighteenth century by organized religion. In every country, Catholic, Protestant and Orthodox alike, even ecclesiastical reformers took it for granted that religion should be upheld and protected by the law and the coercive apparatus of the state. Only a

very few advanced thinkers questioned this. In much of Europe there was still no toleration for views other than those of the established Church. The coronation oath taken by a French king imposed on him the obligation to stamp out heresy, and only in 1787 did non-Catholics in France gain any recognized civic status and therefore the right to legitimize their children by contracting legal marriage. In Catholic countries the censorship, though often far from effective, was still supposed and sometimes strove to prevent the dissemination of writings inimical to Christian belief and the authority of the Church. Although the Counter-Reformation spirit had ebbed and the Jesuits were dissolved, the Index of prohibited books and the Inquisition which had first compiled it were maintained. The universities everywhere were in clerical hands; even in England, Oxford and Cambridge were closed to nonconformist dissenters and Roman Catholics. Religion also largely determined the content of their teaching and the definition of the studies they pursued.

THE GROWTH OF NEW INSTITUTIONS

The institutional fabric of society also showed the onset of innovation. One of the reasons why universities lost importance in these centuries was that they no longer monopolized the intellectual life of Europe. From the middle of the seventeenth century there appeared in many countries, and often under the highest patronage, academies and learned societies such as the English Royal Society, which was given a charter in 1662, or the French Académie des Sciences, founded four years later. In the eighteenth century such associations greatly multiplied; they were diffused through smaller towns and founded with more limited and special aims,

In a manuscript dating from c.1532, Francis I, King of France and patron of literature and the arts, is depicted being presented with a translation of works by Diodore of Sicily.

Freemasons gather to discuss the exposure of a fraud in their midst. This meeting was held at a London Masonic lodge in 1786, at a time when Masonic membership was rising fast.

such as the promotion of agriculture. A great movement of voluntary socialization was apparent; though most obvious in England and France, it left few countries in Western Europe untouched. Clubs and societies of all sorts were a characteristic of an age no longer satisfied to exhaust its potential in the social institutions of the past, and they sometimes attracted the attention of government. Some of them made no pretension to have as their sole end literary, scientific or agricultural activity, but provided gatherings and meeting-places at which general ideas were debated, discussed or merely chatted about. In this way they assisted the circulation of new ideas. Among such associations the most remarkable was the international brotherhood of Freemasons. It was introduced from England to continental Europe in the 1720s and within a half-century spread widely;

there may have been more than a quarter-million Masons by 1789. They were later to be the object of much calumny; the myth was propagated that they had long had revolutionary and subversive aims. This was not true of the craft as a body, however true it may have been of a few individual Masons, but it is easy to believe that so far as Masonic lodges, like other gatherings, helped in the publicity and discussion of new ideas, they contributed to the breaking up of the ice of tradition and convention.

LITERACY

THE INCREASED CIRCULATION of ideas and information did not, of course, rest primarily on meetings held by clubs and societies, but on the diffusion of the written word through print. One of the crucial transformations of Europe after 1500 was that it became more literate; some have summed it up as the change from a culture focused on the image to one focused on the word. Reading and writing (and especially the former), though not universally diffused, had, nevertheless, become widespread and in some places common. They were no longer the privileged and arcane knowledge of a small élite, nor were they any longer mysterious in being intimately and specially connected with religious rites.

In assessing this change we can emerge a little way from the realm of imponderables and enter that of measurable data which shows that somehow, for all the large pools of illiteracy which still existed in 1800, Europe was by then a literate society as it was not in 1500. That is, of course, not a very helpful statement as it stands. There are many degrees of attainment in both reading and writing. Nevertheless, however we define our terms, Europe and its dependencies in 1800 probably contained most of the literate people in the world. It therefore had a higher proportion of literates than other cultures. This was a critical historical change. By then, Europe was well into the age of the predominance of print, which eventually superseded, for most educated people, the spoken word and images as the primary means of instruction and direction, and lasted until the twentieth century restored oral and visual supremacy by means of radio, cinema and television.

DIFFERING LEVELS OF LITERACY

The sources for assessing literacy are not good until the middle of the nineteenth century – when, it appears, somewhere about half of all Europeans still could neither read nor write – but they all suggest that the improvement from about 1500 was cumulative but uneven. There were important differences between countries, between the same countries at different periods, between town and country, between the sexes, and between occupations. All this is still true, though in diminished degree, and it greatly simplifies the problem of making general statements: none but the vaguest are possible until recent times. But specific facts are suggestive about trends.

The first signs of the educational effort underlying the increase of literacy can be seen before the invention of printing. They appear to be another part of that revival and invigoration of urban life between the twelfth and

This painting of a graduation ceremony at the University of Leyden in the Netherlands dates from 1649. By that time, the social promotion that knowledge could bring meant that a good education was a valuable asset.

thirteenth centuries whose importance has already been noted. Some of the earliest evidence of the commissioning of school-masters and provision of school places comes from the Italian cities which were then the vanguard of European civilization. In them there soon appeared a new appreciation, that literacy is an essential qualification for certain kinds of office. We find, for example, provisions that judges should be able to read, a fact with interesting implications for the history of earlier times.

The early lead of the Italian cities had given way by the seventeenth century to that of England and the Netherlands (both countries with, for the age, a high level of urbanization). These have been thought to be the European countries with the highest levels of literacy in about 1700; the transfer of leadership to them illustrates the way in which the history of rising literacy is geographically an uneven business. Yet French was to be the international language of eighteenth-century

publication and the bedrock of the public which sustained this must surely have been found in France. It would not be surprising if levels of literacy were higher in England and the United Provinces, but the numbers of the literate may well have been larger in France, where the total population was so much bigger.

PRINTING AND THE REFORMATION

An outstanding place in the overall trend to literacy must surely be given to the spread of printing. By the seventeenth century there was in existence a corpus of truly popular publishing, represented in fairy-stories, tales of true and unrequited love, almanacs and books of astrology, and hagiographies. The existence of such material is evidence of demand. Printing had given a new point to being literate, too, for the consultation of manuscripts had

Popular entertainment, such as theatre, was aided by the rise in literacy and the dissemination of printed matter. A performance of Molière's *Le Malade imaginaire* is depicted in this engraving dated 1673.

The first known edition of *El ingenioso hidalgo don Quijote de la Mancha*, the cover of which is shown here, was printed by Juan de la Cueva in Madrid in 1605. The work of a little-known writer called Miguel de Cervantes (1547–1616), *Don Quijote* was to bring its author long-lasting fame, but not wealth.

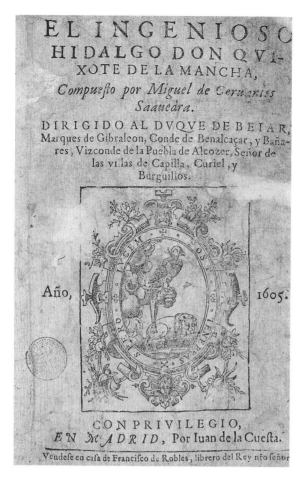

was a great force for enlightenment; it was both a stimulus to reading and a focus for intellectual activity. In England and Germany its importance in the making of a common culture can hardly be exaggerated, and in each country it produced a translation of the Bible which was a masterpiece.

EDUCATION AND PUBLICATIONS

As the instance of the reformers shows, authority was often in favour of greater literacy, but this was not confined to the Protestant countries. In particular, the legislators of innovating monarchies in the eighteenth century often strove to promote education – which meant in large measure primary education. Austria and Prussia were notable in this respect. Across the Atlantic the puritan tradition had from the start imposed in the New England communities the obligation to provide schooling. In other countries education was left to the informal and unregulated operation of private enterprise and charity (as in England), or to the Church. From the sixteenth century begins the great age of particular religious orders devoted to teaching (as in France).

An important consequence, promoter and concomitant of increased literacy was the rise of the periodical press. From broadsheets and occasional printed newsletters there evolved by the eighteenth century journals of regular publication. They met various needs. Newspapers began in seventeenth-century Germany, a daily coming out in London in 1702, and by the middle of the century there was an important provincial press and millions of newspapers were being printed each year. Magazines and weekly journals began to appear in England in the first half of the eighteenth century and the most important of them, the *Spectator*, set a model for journal-

necessarily been difficult and time-consuming, because of their relative inaccessibility. Technical knowledge could now be made available in print very quickly and this meant that it was in the interest of the specialist to read in order to maintain his skill in his craft.

Another force making for literacy was the Protestant Reformation. Almost universally, the reformers themselves stressed the importance of teaching believers how to read; it is no coincidence that Germany and Scandinavia both reached higher levels of literacy than many Catholic countries by the nineteenth century. The Reformation made it important to read the Bible and it had rapidly become available in print in the vernaculars which were thus strengthened and disciplined by the diffusion and standardization which print brought with it. Bibliolatry, for all its more obviously unfortunate manifestations,

ism by its conscious effort to shape taste and behaviour. Here was something new. Only in the United Provinces did journalism have such success as in England; probably this was because all other European countries enjoyed censorships of varying degrees of efficacy as well as different levels of literacy. Learned and literary journals appeared in increasing numbers, but political reporting and comment were rarely available. Even in eighteenth-century France it was normal for the authors of works embodying advanced ideas to circulate them only in manuscript; in this stronghold of critical thought there was still a censorship, though one arbitrary and unpredictable and, as the century wore on, less effective in its operation.

THE "DANGERS" OF LITERACY

It may have been a growing awareness of the subversive potential of easily accessible journalism which led to a change of wind in official attitudes to education. Until the eighteenth century there was no very widespread feeling that education and literacy might be dangerous and should not be widely extended. Though formal censorship had always been a recognition of the potential dangers brought by literacy, there was a tendency to see this in predominantly religious terms; one duty of the Inquisition was to maintain the effectiveness of the Index. In retrospect it may well seem that the greater opportunity which literacy and printing gave for the criticism and questioning of authority in general was a more important effect than their subversion of religion. Yet this was not their only importance. The diffusion of technical knowledge also accelerated other kinds of social change. Industrialization would hardly have been possible without greater literacy and a part of what has been called a

"scientific revolution" in the seventeenth century must be attributed to the simple cumulative effect of more rapidly and widely circulated information.

THE SCIENTIFIC REVOLUTION

THE FUNDAMENTAL SOURCES of the "scientific revolution" lie deeper than the increased availability of information, in changed intellectual attitudes. Their core was a changed view of man's relation to nature. From a natural world observed with bemused awe as evidence of God's mysterious ways, human beings somehow made the great step

This painting by Dutch artist Adriaen van Ostade (1610–1685) depicts a village schoolmaster and his pupils.

*T*he *Alchemist at Work* is portrayed by David Teniers the Elder (1582–1649). Alchemy first emerged in ancient China, India and Greece, and became widespread in medieval Europe. The science of alchemy – more than merely the search for a means to turn base metal into gold (although in that debased form it became notorious) – was the forerunner of chemistry, and alchemists made some important findings, including the discovery of mineral acids and alcohol.

to a conscious search for the means to achieve its manipulation. Although the work of medieval scientists had been by no means as primitive and uncreative as it was once the fashion to believe, it suffered from two critical limitations. One was that it could provide very little knowledge that was of practical use. This inhibited attention to it. The second was its theoretical weakness; it had to be surpassed at a conceptual as well as a technical level. In spite of its beneficial irrigation by ideas from Arab sources and a healthy emphasis on definition and diagnosis in some of its branches, medieval science rested on assumptions which were untested, in part because the means of testing them could not be grasped, in part because the wish to test them did not exist. The dogmatic assertion of the theory that the four elements, Fire, Air, Earth and Water, were the constituents of all things, for example, went unrefuted by experiment. Although experimental work of a sort went on within the alchemical and hermetic traditions, and with Paracelsus came to be directed towards other ends than a search for gold, it was still directed by mythical, intuitive conceptions.

DESCRIPTIVE STUDIES

The tendency to rely on medieval scientific assumptions continued until the seventeenth century. The Renaissance had its scientific manifestations but they found expression usually in descriptive studies (an outstanding example was that of Vesalius' human anatomy of 1543) and in the solution of practical problems in the arts (such as those of perspective) and mechanical crafts. One branch of this descriptive and classificatory work was particularly impressive, that addressed to making sense of the new geographical knowledge revealed by the discoverers and cosmographers. In geography, said a French physician of the early sixteenth century, "and in what pertains to astronomy, Plato, Aristotle, and the old philosophers made progress, and Ptolemy added a great deal more. Yet, were one of them to return today, he would find geography changed past recognition." Here was one

of the stimuli for a new intellectual approach to the world of nature.

It was not a stimulus quick to operate. A tiny minority of educated men, it is true, would already in 1600 not have found it easy to accept the conventional world picture based on the great medieval synthesis of Aristotle and the Bible. Some of them felt an uneasy loss of coherence, a sudden lack of bearings, an alarming uncertainty. But for most of those who considered the matter at all, the old picture still held true, the whole universe still centred on the earth, and the life of the earth upon human beings, its only

Only a century or so after Raphael (1483–1520) painted *The School of Athens (Philosophy)* in the Vatican, the classical world-view would prove inadequate as knowledge became ever more sophisticated and based on rational, observed truths.

rational inhabitants. The greatest intellectual achievement of the next century was to make it impossible for educated people to think like this. It was so important that it has been seen as the essential change to the modern from the medieval world.

FRANCIS BACON

Early in the seventeenth century something new is already apparent in science. The changes which then manifested themselves meant that an intellectual barrier was crossed and the nature of civilization was altered for ever. There appeared in Europe a new

The English statesman and philosopher Francis Bacon (1561–1626) is depicted in this anonymous 17th-century portrait.

attitude, deeply utilitarian, encouraging the curious to invest time, energy and resources to master nature by systematic experiment. When a later age came to look back for its precursors in this attitude they found the outstanding one to have been Francis Bacon, sometime Lord Chancellor of England, fondly supposed by some later admirers to be the author of the plays of Shakespeare, a man of outstanding intellectual energy and many unlikeable personal traits. His works seem to have had little or no contemporary effect but they attracted posterity's attention for what seemed a prophetic rejection of the authority of the past. Bacon advocated a study of nature based upon observation and induction and directed towards harnessing it for human purposes. "The true and lawful end of the sciences," he wrote, "is that human life be enriched by new discoveries and powers." Through them could be achieved a "restitution and reinvigorating [in great part] of man to the sovereignty and power ... which he had in his first state of creation". This was ambitious indeed – nothing less than the redemption of mankind from the consequences of Adam's Fall – but Bacon was sure it was possible if scientific research was effectively organized; in this, too, he was a prophetic figure, precursor of later scientific societies and institutions.

The modernity of Bacon was later exaggerated and other men – notably his contemporaries Kepler and Galileo – had much more to say which was of importance in the advance of science. Nor did his successors adhere so closely as he would have wished to a programme of practical discovery of "new arts, endowments, and commodities for the bettering of man's life" (that is, to a science dominated by technology). Nevertheless, he rightly acquired something of the status of a mythological figure because he went to the heart of the matter in his advocacy of observation and experiment instead of deduction from a priori principles. Appropriately, he is said even to have achieved scientific martyrdom, having caught cold while stuffing a fowl with snow one freezing March day, in order to observe the effects of refrigeration upon the flesh. Forty years later, his central ideas were the commonplace of scientific discourse. "The management of this great machine of the world," said an English scientist in the 1660s, "can be explained only by the experimental and mechanical philosophers." Here were ideas which Bacon would have understood and approved and which are central to the world which we still inhabit. Ever since the seventeenth century it has been a characteristic of the scientist that he answers questions by means of experiment and for a long time it was to lead to new attempts to understand what was revealed by these experiments by constructing systems.

EXPERIMENTAL METHOD

The use of experimentation led at first to concentration on the physical phenomena which could best be observed and measured by the techniques available. Technological innovation had arisen from the slow accretion of skills by European workmen over centuries; these skills could now be directed to the solution of problems which would in turn permit the solution of other, intellectual problems. The invention of logarithms and calculus was a part of an instrumentation which had among other components the building of better clocks and optical instruments. When the clockmaker's art took a great stride forward with the seventeenth-century introduction of the pendulum as a controlling device it in turn made the measurement of time by precision instruments, and therefore astronomy, much easier. With the telescope came new opportunities to scrutinize the heavens; Harvey discovered the circulation of the blood as the result of a theoretical investigation by experiment, but *how* circulation took place was only made comprehensible when the microscope made it possible to see the tiny vessels through which blood flowed. Telescopic and microscopic observation were not only central to the

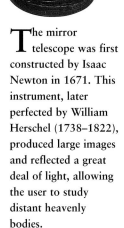

The mirror telescope was first constructed by Isaac Newton in 1671. This instrument, later perfected by William Herschel (1738–1822), produced large images and reflected a great deal of light, allowing the user to study distant heavenly bodies.

Microscopes, such as this late 18th-century model, made possible the study of major new scientific fields. For example, with the discovery of the existence of "animalcules" – infinitesimally minute living creatures, later called bacteria – microbiology was born.

Chemistry

Chemistry was a practical subject which perfected the use of metals and their alloys, dyes, pottery, gunpowder, salts and many other substances. It was in the field of alchemy, in which outstanding Arab achievements were followed in the 16th century by the Western alchemists, that investigation of such topics began. Modern chemistry began in the 17th century, along with new methods, knowledge and definitions, expounded by scientists such as Robert Boyle, Johann Glauber, Jean-Baptiste van Helmont, Friedrich Hoffmann, Wilhelm Homberg, Johan Kunckel, Nicolas Lémery and Jean Rey. In the 18th century, thanks to the work of Antoine Lavoisier, chemical theory was born and fundamental laws began to be grasped.

An 18th-century chemistry laboratory is shown in an engraving from Diderot's Encyclopédie.

discoveries of the scientific revolution, moreover, but made visible to laymen something of what was implied in a new world outlook.

THE NEW SCIENTIFIC COMMUNITY

What was not achieved for a long time was the line of demarcation between the scientist and philosopher which we now recognize. Yet a new world of scientists had come into being, a true scientific community and an international one, too. Here we come back to printing. The rapid diffusion of new knowledge was very important. The publication of scientific books was not its only form; the *Philosophical Transactions* of the Royal Society were published and so were, increasingly, the memoirs and proceedings of other learned bodies. Scientists moreover kept up voluminous private correspondences with one another, and much of the material they recorded in them has provided some of the most valuable evidence for the way in which scientific revolution actually occurred. Some of these correspondences were published; they were more widely intelligible and read than would be the exchanges of leading scientists today.

One feature of the scientific revolution remarkable to the modern eye is that it was something in which amateurs and part-time enthusiasts played a big part. It has been suggested that one of the most important facts explaining why science progressed in Europe while stagnation overtook even outstanding technical achievement in China, was the association with it in Europe of the social prestige of the amateur and the gentleman.

The membership of the learned societies which began to appear more widely at about the mid-seventeenth century was full of gentlemanly dabblers who could not by any stretch of imagination have been called professional scientists but who lent to these bodies the indefinable but important weight of their standing and respectability whether or not they got their hands dirty in experimental work.

LIMITATIONS

By 1700 specialization between the major different branches of science already existed though it was by no means as important as it was to become. Nor was science in those days relentlessly demanding on time; scientists could still make major contributions to their study while writing books on theology or holding administrative office. This suggests some of the limitations of the seventeenth-century revolution; it could not transcend the limits of the techniques available and while they permitted great advances in some fields, they tended to inhibit attention to others. Chemistry, for example, made relatively small progress (though few still accepted the Aristotelian scheme of four elements which had still dominated thinking about the constituents of matter in 1600), while physics and cosmology went ahead rapidly and indeed arrived at something of a plateau of consolidation which resulted in less spectacular but steady advance well into the nineteenth century, when new theoretical approaches reinvigorated them.

SCIENCE AND GOD

Altogether, the seventeenth-century scientific achievement was a huge one. First and

foremost, it replaced a theory of the universe which saw phenomena as the direct and often unpredictable operation of divine power by a conception of it as a mechanism, in which change proceeded regularly from the uniform and universal working of laws of motion. This was still quite compatible with belief in God. His majesty was not perhaps shown in daily direct intervention but in his creation of a great machine; in the most celebrated analogy God was the great watch-maker. Neither the typical student of science nor the scientific world view of the seventeenth century was anti-religious or anti-theocentric. Though it was indubitably important that new views on astronomy, by displacing human beings from the centre of the universe, implicitly challenged their uniqueness (it was in 1686 that a book appeared arguing that there might be more than one inhabited world), this was not what preoccupied the men who made the cosmological revolution. For them it was only an accident that the authority of the Church became entangled with the proposition that the sun went round the earth. The new views they put forward

The English artist Joseph Wright (1734–1797) specialized in scientific subjects. In this painting, entitled *An Experiment on a Bird in an Air-pump*, he depicts a physicist creating a vacuum. Wright's work illustrates the growing fashion in élite circles for public scientific demonstrations.

merely emphasized the greatness and mysteriousness of God's ways. They took for granted the possibility of christening the new knowledge as Aristotle had been christened by the Middle Ages.

THE COPERNICAN UNIVERSE

The great roll of the cosmological revolution has always been headed by the name of Copernicus, a Polish cleric whose book *On the Revolutions of the Celestial Orbs* was published in 1543. This was the same year as Vesalius' great work on anatomy (and, curiously, of the first edition of the works of Archimedes); Copernicus was a Renaissance humanist rather than a scientist – not surprisingly, considering when he lived. In part for philosophic and aesthetic reasons he hit upon the idea of a universe of planets moving round the sun, explaining their motion as a system of cycles and epicycles. It was (so to speak) a brilliant guess, for he had no means of testing the hypothesis and most common-sense evidence told against it.

Tycho Brahe (1546–1601), the Danish astronomer for whom King Frederick II built an observatory, is depicted in this engraving dated 1586.

The first true scientific data in support of heliocentricity was in fact provided by a man who did not accept it, the Dane Tycho Brahe. Besides possessing the somewhat striking distinction of an artificial nose, Brahe began recording the movements of planets, first with rudimentary instruments and then, thanks to a munificent king, from the best-equipped observatory of his age. The result was the first systematic collection of astronomical data to be made within the orbit of the Western tradition since the Alexandrian era. Kepler, the first great Protestant scientist, who was invited by Brahe to assist him, went on to make even more careful observations of his own and provide a second major theoretical step forward. He showed that the movements of planets could be explained as regular if their courses followed ellipses at irregular speeds. This broke at last with the Ptolemaic framework within which cosmology had been more and more cramped and provided the basis of planetary explanation until the

Nicholas Copernicus (1473–1543), the Polish theologian, astronomer and mathematician, caused a great scandal when he asserted that the earth rotated round the sun once a year, and on its own axis once a day.

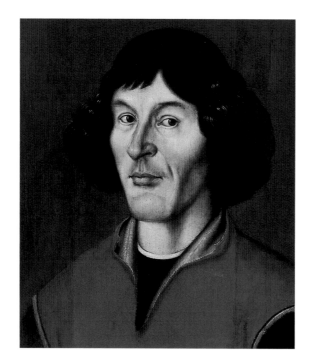

twentieth century. Then came Galileo Galilei, who eagerly seized upon the telescope, an instrument seemingly discovered about 1600, possibly by chance. Galileo was an academic, professor at Padua of two subjects characteristically linked in early science: physics and military engineering. His use of the telescope finally shattered the Aristotelian scheme; Copernican astronomy was made visible and the next two centuries were to apply to the stars what was known of the nature of the planets.

GALILEO

Galileo's major work was not in observation but in theory. He first described the physics which made a Copernican universe possible by providing a mathematical treatment of the movement of bodies. With his work, mechanics left the world of the craftsman's knowhow, and entered that of science. What is more, Galileo came to his conclusions as a result of systematic experiment. On this rested what Galileo called "two new sciences", statics and dynamics. The published result was the book in which has been seen the first statement of the revolution in scientific thought, Galileo's *Dialogue on the Two Great Systems of the World* (that of Ptolemy and that of Copernicus) of 1632. Less remarkable than its contents, but still interesting, are the facts that it was written not in Latin but in the vernacular Italian, and dedicated to the pope; Galileo was undoubtedly a good Catholic. Yet the book provoked an uproar, rightly, for it meant the end of the Christian–Aristotelian world view which was the great cultural triumph of the medieval Church. Galileo's trial followed. He was condemned and recanted, but this did not diminish the effect of his work. Copernican views henceforth dominated scientific thinking.

ISAAC NEWTON

In the year that Galileo died, Newton was born. It was his achievement to provide the physical explanation of the Copernican universe; he showed that the same mechanical laws explained both what Kepler and what Galileo had said, and finally brought together terrestrial and celestial knowledge. He employed a new mathematics, the "method of fluxions" or, in later terminology, the infinitesimal calculus. Newton did not invent this; he applied it to physical phenomena. It provided a way of calculating the positions of bodies in motion. His conclusions were set out in a discussion of the movements of the

The Italian astronomer and physicist Galileo Galilei (1564–1642), who was forced publicly to recant his heretical views under threat of torture from the Inquisition, is portrayed in this contemporary painting.

planets contained in a book which was the most important and influential scientific work since that of Euclid. The *Principia*, as it is called for short (or, anglicized, *The Mathematical Principles of Natural Philosophy*), demonstrated how gravity sustained the physical universe. The general cultural consequences of this discovery were comparable with those within science. We have no proper standard of measurement, but perhaps they were even greater. That a single law, discovered by observation and calculation, could explain so much was an astonishing revelation of what the new scientific thinking could achieve. Pope has been quoted to excess, but his epigram still best summarizes the impact of Newton's work on educated society:

Nature and Nature's laws lay hid in night:
God said, "Let Newton be!" and all was light.

Newton thus in due time became, with Bacon, the second of the canonized saints of a New Learning. There was little exaggeration in this in Newton's case. He was a man of almost universal scientific interests and, as the phrase has it, touched little that he did not adorn. Yet the significance of much of what Newton did is bound to elude the non-scientist. Manifestly, he completed the revolution begun with Copernicus. A dynamic conception of the universe had replaced a static one. His achievement was great enough to provide the physics of the next two centuries and to underpin all the other sciences with a new cosmology.

THE CONFLICT OF SCIENCE AND RELIGION

WHAT WAS NOT ANTICIPATED by Newton and his predecessors was that their work might presage an insoluble conflict of science and religion. Newton, indeed, seems even to have been pleased to observe that the law of gravity did not adequately sustain the view that the universe was a self-regulated system, self-contained once created; if it was not just a watch, its creator could do more than invent it, build it, wind it up and then stand back. He welcomed the logical gap which he could fill by postulating divine intervention, for he was a passionate Protestant apologist. Churchmen, especially Catholic, nevertheless did not find it easy to come to terms with the new science. In the Middle Ages clerics had made important contributions to science, but from the seventeenth to the mid-nineteenth century, very little first-rank scientific work was done by churchmen. This was truer, certainly, of the countries where the Counter-Reformation had triumphed than those where it had not. In the seventeenth century there opened that split between organized religion and science which has haunted European intellectual history ever since, whatever efforts have from time to time been made to patch it up. The symbolic crisis was that of the Neapolitan Bruno. He was not a scientist but a speculator, formerly a Dominican monk who broke with his order and wandered about Europe publishing controversial works, dabbling in a magical "secret science" supposedly derived from ancient Egypt. In the end the Inquisition took him and after eight years in its hands he was burned at Rome for heresy. His execution became one of the foundations of the later historical mythology of the development of "free thought", of the struggle between progress and religion as it was to come to be seen.

DEFENDERS OF RELIGIOUS BELIEF AND THE CHURCH

In the seventeenth century an antithesis between progress and religion was not much felt by scientists and philosophers. Newton, who wrote copiously on biblical and theological topics and believed his work on the prophetical books to be as flawless as the *Principia*, seems to have held that Moses knew about the heliocentric theory and recommended his readers to "beware of Philosophy and vain deceit and oppositions of science falsely so called" and to have recourse to the Old Testament. Napier, the inventor of logarithms, was delighted to have in them a new tool to deploy in deciphering the mysterious references in the Book of Revelation to the Number of the Beast. The French philosopher Descartes formulated what he found to be satisfactory philosophical defences of religious belief and Christian truth coherent with his technically sceptical approach to his subject. This did not prevent him (or the philosophical movement which took its name from him, Cartesianism) from attracting the hostility of the Church. The

traditional defenders of religious belief correctly recognized that what was at stake was not only the conclusions people arrived at, but the way that they arrived at them. A rationally argued acceptance of religious belief which started from principles of doubt and demonstrated they could satisfactorily be overcome was a poor ally for a Church which taught that truth was declared by Authority. The Church was quite right in setting aside as irrelevant Descartes' own devotion and Christianity and correctly (from its own point of view) put all his works on the Index.

The argument from authority was taken up by a French Protestant clergyman of the

The occasional co-existence of scientific experimentation, religion and superstition is demonstrated in this 18th-century painting by Joseph Wright entitled *The Alchymist, in Search of the Philosopher's Stone, Discovers Phosphorus, and Prays for the Successful Conclusion of his Operation, as was the custom of the Ancient Chymical.*

The German philosopher Immanuel Kant is portrayed in this 18th-century lithograph.

later seventeenth century, Pierre Bayle, who pointed out that it had an unsatisfactory open-endedness. What authority prescribed the authority? In the end it seemed to be a matter of opinion. Every dogma of traditional Christianity, he suggested, might be refuted if not in accordance with natural reason. With such ideas a new phase in the history of European thought announced itself; it has been called the Enlightenment.

THE ENLIGHTENMENT

THE WORD ENLIGHTENMENT and similar ones were used in the eighteenth century in most European languages to characterize the thinking which Europeans felt distinguished their own age and cut it off from what had gone before. The key image is of the letting in of light upon what was dark, but when the German philosopher Kant asked the question "What is enlightenment?" in a famous essay he gave a different answer: liberation from self-imposed tutelage. At its heart lay a questioning of authority. The great heritage to be left behind by the Enlightenment was the generalizing of the critical attitude. From this time, everything was exposed to scrutiny. Some felt – and it came in the very long run to be true – that nothing was sacred, but this is somewhat misleading. Enlightenment had its own authority and dogmas; the critical stance itself long went unexamined. Furthermore, Enlightenment was as much a bundle of attitudes as a collection of ideas and here lies another difficulty in coming to terms with it. Many streams flowed into this result but by no means did they all follow the same course. The roots of Enlightenment are as confused as its development, which always resembled a continuing debate – sometimes a civil war – much more than the advance of a united army of the enlightened.

Descartes had taught men that systematic doubt was the beginning of firm knowledge. Fifty years later, the English philosopher John Locke provided an account of the psychology of knowledge which reduced its primary constituents to the impressions conveyed by the senses to the mind; there were not, he argued against Descartes, ideas innate in human nature. The mind contained only sense-data and the connexions it made between them. This was, of course, to imply that humanity had no fixed ideas of right and wrong; moral values, Locke taught, arose as the mind experienced pain and pleasure. There was to be an enormous future for the development

Kant's *What is Enlightenment?*

"For enlightenment of this kind, all that is needed is *freedom* ... freedom to make *public use* of one's reason in all matters. But I hear on all sides the cry: *Don't argue*! The officer says: Don't argue, get on parade! The tax-official: Don't argue, pay! The clergyman: Don't argue, believe! ... All this means restrictions on freedom everywhere. ... But by the public use of one's own reason I mean that use which anyone may make of it *as a man of learning* addressing the entire *reading public*. ... Thus it would be very harmful if an officer receiving an order from his superiors were to quibble openly, while on duty ... . He must simply obey. But he cannot reasonably be banned from making observations as a man of learning on the errors in the military service, and from submitting these to his public for judgement. The citizen cannot refuse to pay the taxes imposed upon him; presumptuous criticisms of such taxes ... may be punished as an outrage which could lead to general insubordination. Nonetheless, the same citizen does not contravene his civil obligations if, as a learned individual, he publicly voices his thoughts on the impropriety or even injustice of such fiscal measures."

An extract from *An Answer to the Question: 'What is Enlightenment?'* by Immanuel Kant (1724–1804), translated by H. B. Nisbet.

Descartes' *Discourse on Method*

" ... I believed I would have sufficient in the four following rules, so long as I took a firm and constant resolve never once to fail to observe them.

"The first was never to accept anything as true that I did not know to be evidently so: that is to say, carefully to avoid precipitancy and prejudice, and to include in my judgements nothing more than what presented itself so clearly and distinctly to my mind that I might have no occasion to place it in doubt.

"The second, to divide each of the difficulties that I was examining into as many parts as might be possible and necessary in order best to solve it.

"The third, to conduct my thoughts in an orderly way, beginning with the simplest objects and the easiest to know, in order to climb gradually, as by degrees, as far as the knowledge of the most complex, and even supposing some order among those objects which do not precede each other naturally.

"And the last, everywhere to make such complete enumerations and such general reviews that I would be sure to have omitted nothing."

An extract from *Discourse on Method* (1637) by René Descartes (1596–1650), translated by F. E. Sutcliffe.

of such ideas; from them would flow ideas about education, about society's duty to regulate material conditions and about many other derivations from environmentalism. There was also a huge past behind them: the dualism which Descartes and Locke both expressed in their distinctions of body and mind, physical and moral, have their roots in Plato and Christian metaphysics. Yet what is perhaps most striking at this point is that his ideas could still be associated by Locke with the traditional framework of Christian belief.

AN OPTIMISTIC CREED

Incoherences were always to run through the Enlightenment, but its general trend is clear. The new prestige of science, too, seemed to promise that the observations of the senses were, indeed, the way forward to knowledge, and knowledge whose value was proved by its utilitarian efficacy. It could make possible the improvement of the world in which human beings lived. Its techniques could unlock the mysteries of nature and reveal their logical, rational foundations in the laws of physics and chemistry.

All this was long an optimistic creed (the word *optimistie* entered the French language in the seventeenth century). The world was getting better and would continue to do so. In 1600 things had been very different. Then, the Renaissance worship of the classical past had combined with the upheavals of war and the always latent feeling of religious men that

The German mathematician, rationalist philosopher and logician Gottfried Leibniz (1646–1716) saw evil as the consequence of a series of "misunderstandings". Voltaire invented the term *optimistie* to describe Leibniz, who believed that once such "misunderstandings" were resolved, universal peace would reign.

the end of the world could not long be delayed, to produce a pessimistic mood and a sense of decline from a great past. In a great literary debate over whether the achievements of the ancients excelled those of modern times the writers of the late seventeenth century crystallized the idea of progress which emerged from the Enlightenment. It was also a non-specialists' creed. In the eighteenth century it was still possible for an educated man to tie together in a manner satisfactory at least for himself the logic and implications of many different studies. Voltaire was famous as a poet and playwright, but wrote at length on history (he was for a time the French historiographer royal) and expounded Newtonian physics to his contemporaries. Adam Smith was renowned as a moral philosopher before he dazzled the world with his *Wealth of Nations*, a book which may reasonably be said to have founded the modern science of economics.

RELIGION AND THE ENLIGHTENMENT

In such eclecticism religion, too, found a place, yet (as Gibbon put it) "in modern times, a latent, and even involuntary, scepticism adheres to the most pious disposition". In "enlightened" thought there seemed to be

D'Alembert and philosophy of the Enlightenment era

"Our time likes to call itself 'the era of philosophy'. Indeed, if we examine the current situation of our knowledge, without prejudice, we cannot deny that philosophy has made great progress among us. The science of nature daily acquires new riches, geometry widens its frontiers and carries its torch into the domains of physics, closest to it; at last, the true system of the world is revealed, developed and perfected. The science of nature widens its vision from Earth to Saturn, from the history of the skies to that of insects. And with it, all the other sciences take on new life. But the discovery and use of a new method of philosophy has awakened, however, through the enthusiasm which accompanies all great discoveries, a general increase of ideas. All these causes have contributed to producing a vital effervescence of all spirits. This effervescence, which spreads everywhere, violently attacks anything which stands up to it … . Everything has been discussed, analysed, stirred up, from the principles of science to the fundaments of religion, from the problems of metaphysics to those of taste, from music to morals, from theological questions to those of economy and trade, from politics to civil rights. As the fruit of this general effervescence of spirits, a new light is being shed on many objects and a new darkness covers them, as in the ebb and flow of the tide beaching unexpected things on the shore and pulling others away with it."

The French philosopher and physicist D'Alembert (1717–1783) is depicted in this 18th-century engraving.

An extract from *Essay on the Elements of Philosophy* by Jean le Rond d'Alembert, 1758.

small room for the divine and the theological. It was not just that Europeans no longer felt hell gaping about them and that the world became less mysterious; it also promised to be less tragic. More and more troubles seemed not inseparable from being, but man-made. Awkward problems, it was true, might still be presented by appalling natural disasters such as earthquakes, but if the relief of most ills was possible, if, as one thinker put it, "Man's proper business is to seek happiness and avoid misery", what was the relevance of the dogmas of Salvation and Damnation? God could still be included in a perfunctory way in the philosopher's account of the universe, as the First Cause that had started the whole thing going and the Great Mechanic who prescribed the rules on which it ran, but was there any place for his subsequent intervention in its working, either directly by incarnation or indirectly through his Church and the sacraments it conveyed? Inevitably, the Enlightenment brought revolt against the Church, the supreme claimant to intellectual and moral authority.

Denis Diderot (1713–1784), portrayed here in 1784, was commissioned to direct the *Encyclopédie* (1751–1776), a demonstration of the triumph of the rationalist spirit.

REJECTION OF THE AUTHORITY OF THE PAST

Here was a fundamental conflict. The rejection of authority by thinking individuals in the seventeenth and eighteenth centuries was only rarely complete, in the sense that new authority was sought and discovered in what were believed to be the teachings of science and reason. Yet increasingly and more and more emphatically the authority of the past was rejected. As the literary argument over ancient and modern culture advanced the destruction of the authority of classical teaching, so had the Protestant Reformation exploded the authority of the Catholic Church, the other pillar of traditional European culture. When the Protestant reformers had replaced old priest by new presbyter (or by the Old Testament) they could not undo the work of undermining religious authority which they had begun and which the men of the Enlightenment were to carry much further.

CONFIDENCE IN THE ENLIGHTENMENT

The implications of the Enlightenment took some time to emerge, whatever the quickly formulated and justified misgivings of churchmen. The characteristics of advanced thought in the eighteenth century tended to express themselves in fairly practical and everyday recommendations which in a measure masked their tendency. They are probably best summarized in terms of the fundamental beliefs which underlay them and of which they were consequences. At the basis of all others was a new confidence in the power of mind; this was one reason why the Enlightened so much admired Bacon, who shared this with them, yet even the creative giants of the Renaissance did not do so much to give Europeans a conviction of intellectual power as did the eighteenth century. On this rested the assurance that almost indefinite improvement was possible. Most thinkers of the age were optimists who saw it as the apex of history. Confidently they looked forward to the improvement of the lot of mankind by the manipulation of nature and the unfolding to human beings of the truths which reason had written in their hearts. Innate ideas bundled out by the front door crept in again by the back stairs. Optimism was qualified only by the realization that there were big practical obstacles to be overcome. The first of these was simply ignorance. Perhaps a knowledge of Final Causes was impossible (and certainly science seemed to suggest this as it revealed more and more complexity in nature) but this was not the sort of ignorance which worried the Enlightened. They had a more everyday level of experience in mind and the combination of reason and knowledge gave confidence that ignorance could be dispersed. The greatest literary embodiment of Enlightenment had precisely this aim.

The great *Encyclopédie* of Diderot and D'Alembert was a huge compilation of information and propaganda in twenty-one volumes published between 1751 and 1765. As some of its articles made clear, another great obstacle to enlightenment was intolerance – especially when it interfered with freedom of publication and debate. Parochialism was yet another barrier to happiness. The values of the Enlightenment, it was assumed, were those of all civilized people. They were universal. Never, except perhaps in the Middle Ages, has the European intellectual élite been more cosmopolitan or shared more of a common language. Its cosmopolitanism was increased by knowledge of other societies, for which the Enlightenment showed an extraordinary appetite. In part this was because of genuine curiosity; travel and discovery brought to

These first editions of the encyclopedia compiled by Denis Diderot and Jean le Rond d'Alembert once formed part of Louis XVI's private collection.

Jovellanos on the value of education

"Is it not education which develops intellectual faculties and which increases man's physical strength? Without it, his intellect is like an unlit torch; with it, he illuminates all the kingdoms of nature, discovering the deepest, hidden caverns, and subjects them to his will. Calculations by an inexpert man with dark strength will have little results, but with the help of nature, what methods can he not use? What obstacles can he not remove? What prodigies can he not produce? This is how education improves human beings, the only beings which can be perfected by it, the only ones gifted with the capacity for perfection. This is the greatest gift that he has received from his ineffable Creator. Education prepares him, gives him the means for his welfare and comfort, and is, finally, the basic origin of individual happiness. It is also the origin of public prosperity which can only be understood as the sum of result of the happiness of individuals who make up the social body."

An extract from *A Thesis on Public Education* (1802) by Gaspar de Jovellanos (1744–1811).

Europeans' notice new ideas and institutions and thus made them more aware of social and ethical relativity and provided new grounds for criticism. Above all, a supposedly humane and enlightened China captured the imagination of eighteenth-century Europeans, a fact which perhaps suggests how superficial was their acquaintance with its realities.

THE INSTITUTIONALIZATION OF CRITICISM

Once ignorance, intolerance and parochialism were removed, it was assumed that the unimpeded operation of the laws of nature, uncovered by reason, would promote the reform of society in everyone's interest except that of those wedded to the past by their blindness or their enjoyment of indefensible privilege. The *Lettres persanes* of the French author Montesquieu began the tradition of suggesting that the institutions of existing societies – in his case the laws of France – could be improved by comparison with the laws of nature. In articulating such a programme, the men of the Enlightenment were appointing themselves as the priesthood of a new social order. In their vision of their role as critics and reformers there emerged for the first time a social ideal which has been with us ever since, that of the intellectual. Moralists, philosophers, scholars, scientists already existed; their defining characteristic was specialized competence. What the Enlightenment invented was the ideal of the generalized critical intellect. Autonomous, rational, continuous and universal criticism was institutionalized as never before and the modern intellectual is the outcome.

THE PHILOSOPHERS

The eighteenth century did not use this term. It had the type, but called its exemplars simply "philosophers". This was an interesting adaptation and broadening of a word already familiar; it came to connote not the specialized mental pursuit of philosophical studies but the acceptance of a common outlook and critical stance. It was a term with moral and evaluative tones, used familiarly by enemies as well as friends to indicate also a zeal to propagate the truths revealed by critical insight to a large and lay public. The archetypes were a group of French writers soon lumped together in spite of their differences and referred to as *philosophes*. Their numbers and celebrity correctly suggest the preponderance of France in the central period of Enlightenment thought. Other countries neither produced so many and such conspicuous figures within this tradition, nor did they usually confer such prestige and eminence on those they had. Yet the presiding deities of the early Enlightenment were the English Newton and Locke; it could be reasonably claimed too that the philosopher who expressed the most extreme development of Enlightenment ideals and methods was Bentham, and that its greatest historiographical monument is Gibbon's work. Further north, Scotland had a great eighteenth-century cultural efflorescence and produced in Hume one of the most engaging as well as the most acute of the Enlightenment's technical philosophers, who combined extreme intellectual scepticism with good nature and social conservatism, and in Adam Smith the author of one of the great creative books of modern times. Among Latin countries, Italy was, outside France, most prolific in its contribution to the Enlightenment in spite of the predominance there of the Roman Church. The Italian Enlightenment would be assured of a

remembrance even if it had thrown up only Beccaria, the author of a book which founded penal reform and the criticism of penology and gave currency to one of the great slogans of history, "the greatest happiness of the greatest number". The German Enlightenment was slower to unroll and less productive of figures who won universal acclaim (possibly for linguistic reasons) but produced in Kant a thinker who, if he consciously sought to go beyond the Enlightenment, nevertheless embodied in his moral recommendations much of what it stood for. Only Spain seemed to lag conspicuously. It was not an unfair impression even allowing for the work of one or two enlightened statesmen; Spanish universities

Montesquieu's *The Spirit of the Laws*

"When legislative power is united with executive power in a single person or in a single body of the magistracy, there is no liberty, because one can fear that the same monarch or senate that makes tyrannical laws will execute them tyrannically.

"Nor is there liberty if the power of judging is not separate from legislative power and from executive power. If it were joined to legislative power, the power over the life and liberty of the citizens would be arbitrary, for the judge would be the legislator. If it were joined to executive power, the judge could have the force of an oppressor."

An extract from *The Spirit of the Laws* by Montesquieu, 1748, translated by Anne M. Cohler, Basia C. Miller and Harold S. Stone.

This 18th-century painting portrays the French author and *philosophe* Voltaire at his desk.

Empress Maria Theresia of Austria (1717–1780) is shown with her French-speaking family in 1772. French was the common language of intellectual Europe during the Enlightenment period.

in the eighteenth century were still rejecting Newton.

FRENCH CULTURAL PRIMACY

Important though the work of other nations was for the history of civilization, that of the French struck contemporaries the most forcefully. There were many reasons: a simple one is that people are always fascinated by power and France under Louis XIV had acquired a prestige long to endure. Another reason is the magnificent instrument for the diffusion of French culture which lay to hand in the French language. It was in the eighteenth century the lingua franca of Europe's intellectuals and its people of fashion alike; Maria Theresia and her children used it for their family correspondence and Frederick II wrote (bad) verses in it. A European audience was assured for any book written in French and it seems likely that the success of that language

actually held back cultural advance in the German tongue.

A common language made possible propaganda, discussion and critical comment, but what would actually be achieved by way of practical reform in the short term was bound to depend on political circumstance. Some statesmen attempted to put "enlightened" ideas into practice, because there were coincidences between the interests of states and the aims of philosophers. This was especially apparent when "enlightened despotisms" found themselves running into opposition from vested interest and conservatism. Such conflicts were obvious in the enforcement of educational reform at the expense of the Church inside the Habsburg dominions, or in Voltaire's attacks, written to the brief of a royal minister, on the *parlement* of Paris when it stood in the way of fiscal innovation. Some rulers, like Catherine the Great of Russia, ostentatiously paraded the influence of Enlightenment ideas on their

Dated 1850, this painting is an evocation of Frederick II of Prussia (1712–1786), centre, at lunch at his Sans Souci palace. His guests are depicted as including famous artists and philosophers; the figure on the far right is Voltaire.

legislation. Perhaps the most important and influential impact of such ideas, apart from those of utilitarian reform which were deployed against the Church, was always in educational and economic matters. In France, at least, the economic recommendations of enlightened thinkers made their mark on administration.

ATTACKS ON THE CHURCH

Religious questions drew the attention of the *philosophes* with unique power. The Church and the effects of its teaching were, of course, still inseparable from every side of Europe's life. It was not just that the Church claimed authority in so much, but also that it was

Jean Calas, the French Protestant merchant who was executed in Toulouse in 1762 for heresy, is depicted saying his farewells to his family in an illustration dated 1767.

physically omnipresent as a great corporate interest, both social and economic; it was involved in some measure in every aspect of society to which the attention of reformers might be drawn. Whether it was because the abuse of sanctuary or clerical privilege stood in the way of judicial reform, or mortmain impeded economic improvement, or a clerical monopoly of education encumbered the training of administrators, or dogma prevented the equal treatment of loyal and valued subjects, the Church seemed to find itself always opposing improvement. But this was not all that drew the fire of the *philosophes*. Religion could also lead, they thought, to crime. One of the last great scandals of the era of religious persecution was the execution of a Protestant at Toulouse in 1762 on the charge of converting Catholics to heresy. For this he was tortured, tried, convicted and executed. Voltaire made this a *cause célèbre*. His efforts did not change the law, but it is impossible

not to believe that, for all the violence of feeling which continued to divide Catholic and Protestant in southern France, they made it impossible for such a judicial murder ever to be repeated. Yet France did not give even a limited legal toleration to Protestants until 1787 and then did not extend it to Jews. By that time Joseph II had already introduced religious toleration into his Catholic territories.

THE ENLIGHTENMENT'S LEGACY

The continuing power of the Church suggests an important limit to the practical success of enlightenment. For all its revolutionary power, it had to operate within the still very restrictive institutional and moral framework of the *ancien régime*. Its relationship with despotism was ambiguous: it might struggle against the imposition of censorship or the

practice of religious intolerance in a theocratic monarchy, but could also depend on
despotic power to carry out reform. Nor, it
must be remembered, were enlightened ideas
the only stimulus to improvement. The
English institutions Voltaire admired did not
stem from enlightenment and many changes
in eighteenth-century England owed more to
religion than to "philosophy".

The greatest political importance of the
Enlightenment lay in its legacies to the future.
It clarified and formulated many of the key
demands of liberalism, though here, too, its
legacy is ambiguous, for the men of the
Enlightenment sought not freedom for its
own sake but freedom for the consequences it
would bring. The possibility of contriving
that human beings should be happy on earth
was the key new idea of the eighteenth century; the age may be said, indeed, not merely
to have invented earthly happiness as a feasi-
ble goal but also the thought that it could be
measured (Bentham wrote of a "felicific calculus") and that it could be promoted
through the exercise of reason. Those ideas
all had profound political implications.

ANTI-CLERICALISM

Apart from the invention of the concept of
earthly happiness, the age made its best-
known contribution to the future European
liberal tradition in a more specific and negative form; the Enlightenment created classical
anti-clericalism. Criticism of what the Church
had done led to support for attacks by the
state upon ecclesiastical organizations and
authority. The struggles of Church and State
had many roots other than philosophical, but
could always be presented as a part of a continuing war of enlightenment and rationality
against superstition and bigotry. In particular,
the papacy attracted criticism – or contempt;

Voltaire seems to have once believed that it
would in fact disappear before the end of the
century. The greatest success of the
philosophes in the eyes of their enemies and
of many of their supporters was the papal dissolution of the Society of Jesus.

A few *philosophes* carried their attacks on
the Church beyond institutions to an attack
on religion itself. Out-and-out atheism
(together with deterministic materialism) had
its first serious expression in the eighteenth
century.

But this was unusual. Most of those during the Enlightenment era who thought about
these things were probably sceptical about the
dogmas of the Church, but kept up a vague
theism. Certainly, too, they believed in the
importance of religion as a social force. As

Joseph II of Austria
(1741–1790), whose
coronation banquet in
Frankfurt in 1765 is
shown here, reduced
the power of the
Church, advocated
religious toleration and
abolished serfdom.

Voltaire said, "one must have religion for the sake of the people". He, in any case, continued throughout his life to assert, with Newton, the existence of God and died formally at peace with the Church.

ROUSSEAU

Something always in danger of being lost to sight in the Enlightenment is the importance of the non-intellectual and non-rational side of human nature. The most prophetic figure of the century in this respect and one who quarrelled bitterly with many of the leading figures among the "enlightened" and the *philosophes* was the Genevan Rousseau. His importance in the history of thought lies in his impassioned pleas that due weight be given to the feelings and the moral sense, both in danger of eclipse by rationality. Because of this, he thought, the men of his day were stunted creatures, partial and corrupt beings, deformed by the influence of a

In his *Social Contract* of 1762, the Swiss-born philosopher Jean-Jacques Rousseau (1712–1778) expounded many of the ideas on democracy and government that would later form the basis of the French Revolution. In this engraving dating from the year of his death he is portrayed gathering herbs in Ermenonville.

society which encouraged this eclipse.

European culture owes an enormous amount to Rousseau's vision, much of it to prove pernicious in its effect. He planted (it has been well said) a new torment in every soul. There can be found in his writings a new attitude to religion (which was to revivify it), a new psychological obsession with the individual which was to flood into art and literature, the invention of the sentimental approach to nature and natural beauty, the origins of the modern doctrine of nationalism, a new child-centredness in educational theory, a secularized puritanism (rooted in a mythical view of ancient Sparta), and much else besides. All these things had both good and bad consequences; Rousseau was, in short, the key figure in the making of what has been called Romanticism. In much he was an innovator, and often one of genius. Much, too, he shared with others. His distaste for the Enlightenment erosion of community, his sense that men were brothers and members of a social and moral whole was, for example, expressed just as eloquently by the Irish author Edmund Burke, who nevertheless drew from it very different conclusions. Rousseau was in some measure voicing views beginning to be held by others as the age of Enlightenment passed its zenith. Yet of Rousseau's central and special importance to Romanticism, there can be no doubt.

ROMANTICISM

Romanticism is a much used and much misused term. It can be properly applied to things which seem diametrically opposed. Soon after 1800, for example, some would deny any value to the past and seek to overthrow its legacies just as violently as men of the Enlightenment had done, while at the same time others tenaciously defended historic institutions. Both can be (and have been) called Romantics, because in each of them moral passion counted for more than intellectual analysis. The clearest link between such antitheses lay in the new emphasis of romantic Europe on feeling, intuition, and, above all, the natural. Romanticism, whose expressions were to be so manifold, started almost always from some objection to enlightened thought, whether

The Wanderer Over the Sea of Clouds was painted in 1818 by one of the early European Romantic artists, Caspar David Friedrich (1774–1840).

from disbelief that science could provide an answer to all questions, or from a revulsion against rational self-interest. But its positive roots lay deeper than this, in the Reformation's displacement of so many traditional values by the one supreme value of sincerity; it was not entirely wrong to see Romanticism as some Catholic critics saw it, as a secularized Protestantism, for above all it sought authenticity, self-realization, honesty, moral exaltation. Unhappily it did so all too often without regard to cost. The great effects were to reverberate through the nineteenth century, usually with painful results, and in the twentieth century would affect many other parts of the world as one of the last manifestations of the vigour of European culture.

The Decline of the Carthaginian Empire, by the English painter Joseph Turner (1775–1851), was first exhibited in 1817 and is one of the great masterpieces of the Romantic era.

2 LONG-TERM CHANGE

IN 1798 THOMAS MALTHUS, an English clergyman, published an *Essay on Population* which was to prove the most influential book ever written on the subject. He described what appeared to be the laws of population growth but his book's importance transcended this apparently limited scientific task. Its impact on, for example, economic theory and biological science was to be just as important as the contribution it made to demographic studies. Here, though, such important consequences matter less than the book's status as a symptom of a change in thinking about population. Roughly speaking, for two centuries or so European statesmen and economists had agreed that a rising population was a sign of prosperity. Kings and queens should seek to increase the number of their subjects, it was thought, not merely because this would provide more tax-payers and soldiers but because a bigger population both quickened economic life and was an indication that it had done so. Obviously, larger numbers showed that the economy was providing a living for more people. This view was in its essentials endorsed by no less an authority than the great Adam Smith himself, whose *Wealth of Nations*, a book of huge influence, had agreed as recently as 1776 that an increase in population was a good rough test of economic prosperity.

This illustration, which depicts a busy marketplace at Louth in Lincolnshire, England, dates from the time when Thomas Malthus (1766–1834) was writing about population growth.

THOMAS MALTHUS

Malthus doused the view that population growth signified prosperity with very cold water. Whatever the consequences for society as a whole might be judged to be, he concluded that a rising population sooner or later spelt disaster and suffering for most of its members, the poor. In a famous demonstration he argued that the produce of the earth had finite limits, set by the amount of land available to grow food. This in turn set a limit to population. Yet population always tended to grow in the short run. As it grew, it would press increasingly upon a narrowing margin of subsistence. When this margin was exhausted, famine must follow. The population would then fall until it could be maintained with the food available. This mechanism could only be kept from operating if men and women abstained from having children (and prudence, as they regarded the consequences, might help them by encouraging late marriage) or by such horrors as the natural checks imposed by disease or war.

Much more could be said about the complexity and refinement of this gloomy thesis. It aroused huge argument and counter-argument, and whether true or false, a theory attracting such attention must tell us much about the age. Somehow, the growth of population had begun to worry people so that even prose so unattractive as that of Malthus had great success. People had become aware of population growth as they had not been aware of it before and had done so just as it was to become faster than ever. In the nineteenth century, in spite of what Malthus had said, the numbers of some divisions of

The Scottish economist Adam Smith (1723–1790), whose portrait adorns this 1787 medallion, firmly believed that economic freedom was beneficial for society.

the human race went up with a rapidity and to levels hitherto inconceivable.

POPULATION GROWTH

A LONG VIEW IS BEST for measuring such a change; there is nothing to be gained and much to be lost by worrying about precise dates and the overall trends run on well into the twentieth century. If we include Russia (whose population has until very recent times to be estimated from very poor statistics) then a European population of about one hundred and ninety million in 1800 rose to about four hundred and twenty million a century later. As the rest of the world seems to have grown rather more slowly, this represented a rise in Europe's share of the total population of the world from about one-fifth to one-quarter; for a little while, her disadvantage in numbers by comparison with the great Asiatic centres of population was reduced (while she continued to enjoy her technical and psychological superiority). Moreover, at the same time, Europe was sustaining a huge emigration of her stocks. In the 1830s European emigration overseas first passed the figure of a hundred thousand a year; in 1913 it was over a million and a half. Taking an even longer view, perhaps fifty million people left Europe to go overseas between 1840 and 1930, most of them to the western hemisphere. All these people and their descendants ought to be added to the totals in order to grasp how much European population growth accelerated in these years.

This growth was not shared evenly within Europe and this made important differences to the standing of great powers. Their strength was usually reckoned in terms of military manpower and it was a crucial change that Germany replaced France as the largest mass of population under one government west of Russia in the second half of the nineteenth century. A dramatic increase had been shown earlier in the United Kingdom, whose population grew from about 8 million when Malthus wrote to 22 million by mid-century. It was to reach 36 million by 1914. Another way of looking at such changes would be to compare the respective shares of Europe's population enjoyed by the major military powers at different dates. Between 1800 and 1900, for example, that of Russia grew from 21 to 24 per cent of the total, Germany's from 13 to 14, while France's fell from 15 to 10 per cent, and that of Austria slightly less, from 15 to 12.

FALLING MORTALITY RATES

Population grew everywhere, though at different rates at different times. The poorest agrarian regions of Eastern Europe, for example, experienced their highest growth rates only in the 1920s and 1930s. This is because

the basic mechanism of population increase in this period, underlying change everywhere, was a fall in mortality. Never in history has there been so spectacular a fall in death-rates as in the last hundred years, and it showed first in the advanced countries of Europe in the nineteenth century. Roughly speaking, before 1850 most European countries had birth-rates which slightly exceeded death-rates and both were about the same in all countries. They showed, that is to say, how little impact had been made by that date upon the fundamental determinants of human life in a still overwhelmingly rural society. After 1880 this changed rapidly. The death-rate in advanced European countries fell pretty steadily, from about 35 per thousand inhabitants per year to about 28 by 1900; it would be about 18 fifty years later. Less advanced countries still maintained rates of 38 per thousand between 1850 and 1900, and 32 down to 1950. This produced a striking inequality between two Europes. In the richer, expectation of life was much higher. Since, in large measure, advanced European countries lay in the west, this was (leaving out Spain, a poor country with high mortality) a fresh intensification of older divisions between East and West, a new accentuation of the imaginary line from the Baltic to the Adriatic.

INCREASED LIFE EXPECTANCY

Other factors besides lower mortality helped. Earlier marriage and a rising birth-rate had showed themselves in the first phase of expansion, as economic opportunity increased, but now they mattered much more, since from the nineteenth century onwards, the children of earlier marriages were much more likely to survive, thanks to greater humanitarian concern, cheaper food and

The work of scientists such as Antoine Lavoisier (1743–1794) made possible the medical advances that increased life expectancy. Here, in a drawing by his wife, Lavoisier is shown in his laboratory carrying out research on the human respiratory system.

medical and engineering progress. Of these, medical science and the provision of medical services were the last to influence population trends. Doctors only came to grips with the great killing diseases from about 1870 onwards; these were the child-killers: diphtheria, scarlet fever, whooping-cough, typhoid. Infant mortality was thus dramatically reduced and expectation of life at birth greatly increased. But earlier than this, social reformers and engineers had already done much to reduce the incidence of these and other diseases (though not their fatality) by building better drains and devising better cleaning arrangements for the growing cities. Cholera was eliminated in industrial countries by 1900, though it had devastated London and Paris in the 1830s and 1840s. No Western European country had an important plague outbreak after 1899. As such changes affected more and more countries, their general tendency was everywhere to raise the average age of death with, in the long run, dramatic results. By the second quarter of the twentieth century, men and women in North America, the United Kingdom, Scandinavia and industrial Europe could expect to live two or three times as long as their medieval ancestors. Immense consequences flowed from this.

FAMILY LIMITATION

Just as accelerated population increase first announced itself in those countries which were economically the most advanced, so did the slowing down of growth which was the next discernible demographic trend. This was produced by a declining number of births, though it was for a long time masked because the fall in the death-rate was even faster. In every society this showed itself first among the better-off; to this day, it remains a good

rough working rule that fecundity varies inversely with income (celebrated exceptions among wealthy American political dynasties notwithstanding). In some societies (and in Western rather than Eastern Europe) this was because marriage tended to be put off longer so that women were married for less of their fertile lives; in some it was because couples chose to have fewer children – and could now do so with confidence, thanks to effective contraceptive techniques. Possibly there had long been some knowledge of such techniques in some European countries; it is at least certain that the nineteenth century brought both improvements in them (some made possible by scientific and technical advance in manufacturing the necessary devices) and propaganda which spread knowledge of them. Once more, a social change touches upon a huge ramification of influences, because it is difficult not to connect such spreading knowledge with, for example, greater literacy, and with rising expectations. Although people were beginning to be wealthier than their ancestors, they were all the time adjusting their notion of what was a tolerable life – and therefore a tolerable size of family. Whether they followed the

Entitled *The Origin of the Vaccine*, this contemporary cartoon caricatures Edward Jenner (1749–1823), the pioneer of vaccination. Jenner noticed that people who had suffered from cowpox did not develop the more serious disease smallpox, an observation that led him deliberately to infect subjects with cowpox in order to protect them against smallpox.

calculation by putting off the date of marriage (as French and Irish peasants did) or by adopting contraceptive techniques (as the English and French middle classes seem to have done) was shaped by other cultural factors.

THE EFFECTS OF POPULATION GROWTH

Changes in the ways men and women died and lived in their families transformed the structures of society. On the one hand, the western countries in the nineteenth and twentieth centuries had absolutely more young people about and, for a time, also had them about in a greater proportion than ever before. It is difficult not to think that the expansiveness, buoyancy and vigour of nineteenth-century Europe owed much to this. On the other hand, advanced societies gradually found a much higher percentage of their members surviving into old age than ever before. This increasingly strained the social mechanism which had in earlier centuries maintained the old and those incapable of work; the problem grew worse as competition for industrial employment became more intense. By 1914, in almost every European or North American country much thought had been given to ways of confronting the problems of poverty and dependence, however great the differences in scale and success of efforts to cope with them.

Such trends would not begin to show in Eastern Europe until after 1918, when their general pattern was already well established in the advanced Western countries. Death-rates long continued to fall more sharply than did the birth-rate, even in advanced countries, so that down to the present the population of Europe and the European world has continued to rise. It is one of the most important themes in the history of the era, linked to almost every other. Its material consequences can be seen in unprecedented urbanization and the rise of huge consumer markets for manufacturing industry. The social consequences range from strife and unrest to changing institutions to grapple with them. There were international repercussions as statesmen took into account population figures in deciding what risks they could (and which they had to) take, or as people became more and more alarmed about the consequences of overcrowding. Worries in the nineteenth-century United Kingdom over the prospect of too many poor and unemployed led to the encouragement of emigration which, in its turn, shaped people's thinking and feelings about empire. Later, the Germans discouraged emigration because they feared the loss of military potential, while the French and Belgians pioneered the award of children's allowances for the same reason.

MALTHUS SEEMS TO BE DISPROVED

The introduction of measures designed to influence population levels suggests, correctly, that the gloomy prophecies of Malthus tended to be forgotten as the years went by and the disasters he feared did not take place. The nineteenth century still brought demographic calamities to Europe; Ireland and Russia had spectacular famines and near-famine conditions occurred in many places. But such disaster grew rarer. As famine and dearth were eliminated from advanced countries, this in turn helped to make disease demographically less damaging. Meanwhile Europe north of the Balkans enjoyed two long periods of virtually undisturbed peace from 1815 to 1848 and from 1871 to 1914;

war, another of Malthus' checks, also seemed to be less of a scourge. Finally, his diagnosis actually seemed to be disproved when a rise in population was accompanied by higher standards of living – as rises in the average age of death seemed to show. Pessimists could only reply (reasonably) that Malthus had not been answered; all that had happened was that there had turned out to be much more food available than had been feared. It did not follow that supplies were limitless.

A REVOLUTION IN FOOD PRODUCTION

IN FACT, there was occurring another of those few great changes of history which have decisively transformed the basic conditions of human life. It can reasonably be called a food-producing revolution. Its beginnings have already been traced. In the eighteenth century European agriculture was already capable of obtaining about two and a half times the yield on its seed normal in the Middle Ages. Now even greater agricultural improvement was at hand. Yields would go up to still more spectacular levels. From about 1800, it has been calculated, Europe's agricultural productivity grew at a rate of about one per cent a year, dwarfing all previous advance. More important still, as time passed European industry and commerce would make it possible to tap huge larders in other parts of the world. Both of these changes were aspects of a single process, the accelerating investment in productive capacity which made Europe and North America by 1870 clearly the greatest concentration of wealth on the face of the globe. Agriculture was fundamental to it. People have spoken of an "agricultural revolution" and provided this is not thought of as implying rapid change, it is an acceptable term; nothing

much less strong will describe the huge surge in world output achieved between 1750 and 1870 (and, later, even surpassed). But it was a process of great complexity, drawing on many different sources and linked to the other sectors of the economy in indispensable ways. It was only one aspect of a worldwide economic change which involved in the end not merely continental Europe, but the Americas and Australasia as well.

This illustration from Diderot's *Encyclopédie* (1751–1776) depicts traditional agricultural processes and implements.

Until the latter half of the 19th century, grain was the single most important crop in most of Europe and this is reflected in countless paintings. The English artist John Constable (1776–1837), painted *The Wheatfield* in 1826.

ENGLISH AGRICULTURE

Once important qualifications have been made, it is possible to particularize. By 1750 the best English agriculture was the best in the world. The most advanced techniques were practised and the integration of agriculture with a commercial market economy had gone furthest in England, whose lead was to be maintained for another century or so. European farmers went there to observe methods, buy stock and machinery, seek advice. Meanwhile, the English farmer, benefiting from peace at home (that there were no large-scale and continuous military operations on British soil after 1650 was of literally incalculable benefit to the economy) and a rising population to buy his produce, generated profits which provided capital for further improvement. His willingness to invest them in this way was, in the short run, an optimistic response to the likely commercial prospects but also says something deeper about the nature of English society. The benefits of better farming went in England to individuals who owned their own land or held it securely as leaseholding tenants on terms shaped by market realities. English agriculture was part of a capitalist market economy in which land was even by the eighteenth century treated almost as a commodity like any other. Restraints on its use familiar in European countries had disappeared faster and faster ever since Henry VIII's sequestration of ecclesiastical property. After 1750, the last great stage of this came with the spate of Enclosure Acts at the turn of the century (significantly coincident with high prices for grain) which mobilized for private profit the English peasant's traditional rights to pasture, fuel or other economic benefits. One of the most striking contrasts between English and European agriculture in the early nineteenth century was that the traditional peasant all but disappeared in England. England had wage labourers and smallholders, but the huge European rural populations of individuals with some, if minuscule, legal rights linking them to the soil through communal usages and a mass of tiny holdings, did not exist.

THE TRANSFORMATION OF ENGLISH FARMING METHODS

Inside the framework provided by prosperity and English social institutions, technical progress was continuous. For a long time, much of this was hit-and-miss. Early breeders

of better animals succeeded not because of a knowledge of chemistry, which was in its infancy, or of genetics, which did not exist, but because they backed hunches. Even so, the results were remarkable. The appearance of the livestock inhabiting the landscape changed; the scraggy medieval sheep whose backs resembled, in section, the Gothic arches of the monasteries which bred them, gave way to the fat, square, contented-looking animal familiar today. "Symmetry, well-covered" was an eighteenth-century farmer's toast. The appearance of farms changed as draining and hedging progressed and big, open medieval fields with their narrow strips, each cultivated by a different peasant, gave way to enclosed fields worked in rotation and made a huge patchwork of the English countryside. In some of these fields machinery was at work even by 1750. Much thought was given to its use and improvement in the eighteenth century, but it does not seem that it really made much of a contribution to output until after 1800, when more and more large fields became available, and it became more productive in relation to cost. It was not long before steam engines were driving threshers; with their appearance in English fields, the way was open which would lead

This 19th-century engraving shows a steam-powered threshing machine. Most agricultural tasks, however, were carried out by hand until the late 19th century.

The hard working conditions of the rural peasant are depicted in this painting entitled *Working in the Fields* by the Italian artist Arnaldo Ferraguti (1850–1924). The use of centuries-old farming methods, including three-yearly crop rotation and the fallow field system, continues today in some of the more traditional parts of Europe.

eventually to an almost complete replacement of muscular by machine power on the twentieth-century farm.

new species, and much else. Change on so comprehensive a basis often had to work against the social and political grain, too.

RURAL CHANGE IN CONTINENTAL EUROPE

AGRICULTURAL IMPROVEMENTS and changes spread, *mutatis mutandis* and with a lag in time, to continental Europe. Except by comparison with earlier centuries of quasi-immobility, progress was not always rapid. In Calabria or Andalusia, it might be imperceptible over a century. Nevertheless, rural Europe changed, and the changes came by many routes. The struggle against the inelasticities of food-supply was in the end successful, but it was the outcome of hundreds of particular victories over fixed crop rotations, out-dated fiscal arrangements, poor standards of tillage and husbandry, and sheer ignorance. The gains were better stock, more effective control of plant blight and animal disease, the introduction of altogether

This painting by Francisco de Goya (1748–1828) is entitled *The Grape Harvest*. Intensive farming existed in parts of northern Europe by 1800, but traditional crops and farming methods persisted in most Mediterranean regions, as did the peasant's precarious way of life.

FRANCE

The French formally abolished serfdom in 1789; this probably did not mean much, for

there were few serfs in France at that date. The abolition of the "feudal system" in the same year was a much more important matter. What was meant by this vague term was the destruction of a mass of traditional and legal usages and rights which stood in the way of the exploitation of land by individuals as an investment like any other. Almost at once, many of the peasants who had thought they wanted this discovered that they did not altogether like it in practice; they discriminated. They were happy to abolish the customary dues paid to the lord of the manor, but did not welcome the loss of customary rights to common land. The whole change was made still more confusing and difficult to measure by the fact that there took place at the same time a big redistribution of property. Much land previously belonging to the Church was sold within a few years to private individuals. The consequent increase in the number of people owning land outright and growth in the average size of properties should, on the English analogy, have led to a period of great agricultural advance for France, but it did not. There was very slow progress and little consolidation of properties on the English pattern.

THE GERMANIC LANDS

Generalizations about the pace and uniformity of what was happening should be cautious and qualified. For all the enthusiasm Germans were showing for travelling exhibitions of agricultural machinery in the 1840s, theirs was a huge country and one of those

(France was the other) of which a great economic historian commented that "broadly speaking, no general and thorough-going improvement can be registered in peasant life before the railway age". Yet the dismantling of medieval institutions standing in the way of agricultural improvement did go on steadily before that and prepared the way for it. It was accelerated in some places by the arrival during the Napoleonic period of French armies of occupation which introduced French law, and after this by other forces, so that by 1850 peasants tied to the soil and obligatory labour had disappeared from most of Europe. This did not mean, of course, that attitudes from the *ancien régime* did not linger after its institutions had disappeared. Prussian, Magyar and Polish landlords seem, for good and ill, to have maintained much of their more or less patriarchal authority in the manor even after its legal supports had vanished, and did so as late as 1914. This was important in assuring a continuity of conservative aristocratic values in a much more intense and concentrated way in these areas than in Western Europe. The Junker often accepted the implications of the market in planning his own estate management, but not in his relations with his tenants.

SERFS AND SLAVES

The longest resistance to change in traditional legal forms in agriculture came in Russia. There, serfdom itself persisted until abolished in 1861. This act did not at once bring Russian agriculture entirely under the operation of individualist and market economy principles, but with it an era of European history had closed. From the Urals to Corunna there no longer survived in law any substantial working of land on the basis of serfdom, nor were peasants any longer bound to landlords whom they could not leave. It was the end of a system which had been passed from antiquity to western Christendom in the era of the barbarian invasions and had been the basis of European civilization for centuries. After 1861, Europe's rural proletariat everywhere worked for wages or keep; the pattern which had begun to spread in England and France with the fourteenth-century agricultural crisis had become universal.

Formally, the medieval usage of bond labour lasted longest in some of the American countries forming part of the European world. Obligatory labour in its most unqualified form, slavery, was legal in some of the United States, the most important of these countries, until the end of a great civil war in 1865, when its abolition (though promulgated by the victorious government two years before) became effective throughout the whole republic. The war which had made this possible had been in some measure a distraction from the already rapid development of the country, now to be resumed and to become of vital significance to Europe. Even before the war, cotton-growing, the very agricultural operation which had been the centre of debates over slavery, had already shown how the New World might supplement European agriculture on such a scale as to become almost indispensable. After the war the way was open for the supply to Europe not merely of products such as cotton, which she could not easily grow, but also of food.

ADVANCES IN FOOD DISTRIBUTION

The United States – and Canada, Australia and New Zealand, the Argentine and Uruguay – were soon to show they could offer food at much cheaper prices than

This painting by Claude-Joseph Vernet (1714–1789) shows a road being built through mountainous country-side in France. Improved communications would prove to be a vital factor in the transformation of European agriculture.

Europe herself. Two things made this possible. One was the immense natural resources of these new lands. The American plains, the huge stretches of pasture in the South American pampas and the temperate regions of Australasia provided vast areas for the growing of grain and the raising of livestock. The second was a revolution in transport which made them exploitable for the first time. Steam-driven railways and ships came into service in increasing numbers from the 1860s. These quickly brought down transport costs and did so all the faster as lower prices bred growing demand. Thus further profits were generated to be put into more capital investment on the ranges and prairies of the New World. On a smaller scale the same

phenomenon was at work inside Europe, too. From the 1870s the Eastern European and German farmers began to see that they had a competitor in Russian grain, able to reach the growing cities much more cheaply once railways were built in Poland and western Russia and steamships could bring it from Black Sea ports. By 1900 the context in which European farmers worked, whether they knew it or not, was the whole world; the price of Chilean guano or New Zealand lamb could already settle what went on in their local markets.

Even in such a sketch the story of agricultural expansion bursts its banks; after first creating civilization and then setting a limit to its advance for thousands of years,

The Manchester to Liverpool train is shown transporting cattle, sheep and pigs across northern England in 1831.

The spinning-jenny, a machine that spun and wound yarn on to spindles, was invented by James Hargreaves in 1764. It was to revolutionize the British cotton and wool industries.

agriculture suddenly became its propellant; within a century or so it suddenly demonstrated that it could feed many more people than ever before. The demand of the growing cities, the coming of railways, the availability of capital, all point to its inseparable interconnexion with other sides of a growing transoceanic economy between 1750 and 1870. For all its chronological primacy and its huge importance as a generator of investment capital, the story of agriculture in this period should only for convenience be separated from that of overall growth registered in the most obvious and spectacular way by the appearance of a whole new society, one based on large-scale industrialization.

Curious onlookers gather round George Stephenson's locomotive, the *Rocket*, in 1825. Wagons and rails had been used since ancient times in mining, but the combination of rails, wagons and the locomotive produced something entirely new: the railway.

INDUSTRIALIZATION

INDUSTRIALIZATION is a colossal subject. It is not even easy to see just how big it is. It produced the most striking change in European history since the barbarian invasions, but it has been seen as even more important, as the biggest change in human history since the coming of agriculture, iron or the wheel. Within a fairly short time – a century and a half or so – societies of peasants and craftsmen turned into societies of machine-tenders and bookkeepers. Ironically, it ended the ancient primacy of agriculture from which it had sprung. It was one of the major facts turning human experience back from the differentiation produced by millennia of cultural evolution to common experiences which would tend once more towards cultural convergence.

Even to define it is by no means easy, though the processes which lie at its heart are obvious around us. One is the replacement of human or animal labour by machines driven by power from other, usually mineral, sources. Another is the organization of production in much larger units. Another is the increasing specialization of manufacturing. But all these things have implications and ramifications which quickly take us far beyond them. Although it embodied countless conscious decisions by countless entrepreneurs and customers, industrialization also looks like a blind force sweeping across social life with transforming power, one of the "senseless agencies" a philosopher once detected as half the story of revolutionary

change. Industrialization meant new sorts of towns, needed new schools and new forms of higher learning, even new patterns of daily existence and living together.

SOURCES OF INDUSTRIALIZATION

The roots which made such a change possible go back far beyond the early modern age. Capital for investment had been accumulated slowly over many centuries of agricultural and commercial innovation. Knowledge had been built up, too. Canals were to provide the first network of communication for bulk transport once industrialization got under way, and from the eighteenth century they began to be built as never before in Europe (in China, of course, the story was different). Yet even Charlemagne's men had known how to build them. Even the most startling technical innovations had roots deep in the past. The men of the "Industrial Revolution" (as a Frenchman of the early nineteenth century named the great upheaval of his era) stood on the shoulders of innumerable craftsmen and artificers of pre-industrial times who had slowly built up skills and experience for the future. Fourteenth-century Rhinelanders, for example, learnt to make cast iron; by 1600 the gradual spread of blast furnaces had begun to remove the limits hitherto set to the use of iron by its high cost and in the eighteenth century came the inventions making it possible to use coal instead of wood as fuel for some processes. Cheap iron, even in what were by later standards small quantities, led to experiment with new ways of using it; further changes would then follow. New demand meant that areas where ore was easily to be found became important. When new techniques of smelting permitted the use of mineral rather than vegetable fuel, the location of supplies of coal and iron began to fashion the later industrial geography of Europe and North America. In the northern hemisphere lies much of the discovered coal supply of the world, in a great belt running from the basin of the Don, through Silesia, the Ruhr, Lorraine, the north of England and Wales, to Pennsylvania and West Virginia.

This painting by William Powell Frith (1819–1909) portrays the crowded throng of London's Paddington Station in 1862, a time when the railways were enjoying rapid expansion.

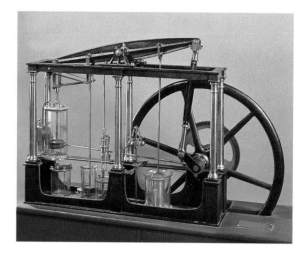

STEAM AND METALLURGY

BETTER METAL AND RICHER FUEL made their decisive contribution to early industrialization with the invention of a new source of energy, the steam engine. Again, the roots are very deep. That the power of steam could be used to produce movement was known in Hellenistic Alexandria. Even if (as some believe) there existed the technology to develop this knowledge, contemporary economic life did not make it worthwhile to strain to do so. The eighteenth century brought a series of refinements so important

that they can be considered as fundamental changes, and did so when there was money to invest in them. The result was a source of power rapidly recognized as of revolutionary importance. The new steam engines were not only the product of coal and iron, they also consumed them, directly both as fuel and as materials used in their own construction. Indirectly they stimulated production by making possible other processes which led to increased demand for them. The most obvious and spectacular was railway-building. It required huge quantities of first iron and then steel for rails and rolling-stock. But it also made possible the movement of objects at much lower cost. What the new trains moved might well again be coal, or ore, thus allowing these materials to be used cheaply far from where they were easily found and dug. New industrial areas followed the lines, from which the railway could carry away goods to distant markets.

THE ADVENT OF STEAM AND OCEAN TRANSPORT

The railway was not the only change steam made to transport and communications. The first steamship went to sea in 1809. By 1870, though there were still many sailing-ships and navies were still building battleships with a full spread of sail, regular ocean sailings by "steamers" were commonplace. The economic effect was dramatic. Oceanic transport's real cost in 1900 was a seventh of what it had been a hundred years earlier. The shrinking of costs, of time spent in transit, and of space, which steamships and railways produced, overturned ideas of the possible. Since the domestication of the horse and the invention of the wheel, people and goods had been conveyed at speeds which certainly varied according to the local roads available, but probably only within limits of no more than one and five miles per hour over any considerable distance. Faster travel was possible on water and this had perhaps increased somewhat over the millennia in which ships underwent quite considerable modification. But all such slow improvement was dwarfed when in a man's lifetime he could witness the difference between travel on horseback and in a train capable of forty or even fifty miles an hour for long periods.

THE GRADUAL APPEARANCE OF FACTORIES

We have now lost one of the most pleasant of industrial sights, the long, streaming plume of steam from the funnel of a locomotive at speed, hanging for a few seconds behind it against a green landscape before disappearing. It greatly struck those who first saw it and so, less agreeably, did other visual aspects of the industrial transformation. One of the most terrifying was the industrial town, dominated by a factory with smoking chimneys, as the pre-industrial town had been by the spire of church or cathedral. So dramatic and novel was the factory, indeed, that it has often gone unremarked that it was an unusual expression of the early stages of industrialization, not a typical one. Even in the middle of the nineteenth century most English industrial workers worked in manufacturing enterprises employing fewer than fifty. For a long time great agglomerations of labour were to be found only in textiles; the huge Lancashire cotton mills which first gave that area a visual and urban character distinct from earlier manufacturing towns were startling because they were unique. Yet by 1850 it was apparent that in more and more manufacturing processes the trend was towards the centralization under one roof made attractive by economies of transport, specialization of function, the use of more powerful machinery and the imposition of effective work discipline.

A contemporary illustration shows the use of steam-powered machinery at an early 19th-century English mine.

This 19th-century painting is entitled *Conference of Engineers at Britannia Bridge, c.1850* and depicts a time when British industrialists and engineers were filled with optimism and pride in their country's technological revolution and led the world with their skill and expertise.

INDUSTRIAL BRITAIN IN THE 19TH CENTURY

In the middle of the nineteenth century the changes of which these were the most striking had only created a mature industrial society in one country, Great Britain. Long and unconscious preparation lay behind this. Domestic peace and less rapacious government than on the continent had bred confidence for investment. Agriculture had provided its new surpluses first in England. Mineral supplies were available to exploit the new technological apparatus resulting from two or three generations of remarkable invention. An expanding overseas commerce generated further profits for investment and the basic machinery of finance and banking was already in being before industrialization needed to call on it and seemed to have readied society psychologically for change; observers detected an exceptional sensitivity to pecuniary and commercial opportunity in eighteenth-century England. Finally, an increasing population was beginning to offer both labour and a rising demand for manufactured goods. All these forces flowed together and the result was unprecedented and continuing industrial growth, first apparent as something totally new and irreversible in the second quarter of the nineteenth century. By 1870 Germany, France, Switzerland, Belgium and the United States had joined Great Britain in showing the capacity for self-sustained economic growth but she was still first among them both in the scale of her industrial plant and in her historic primacy. The inhabitants of "the workshop of the world", as the British liked to think of themselves, were fond of running over the figures which showed how wealth and power had followed upon industrialization. In 1850 the United Kingdom owned half the world's ocean-going ships and contained half the world's railway track. On those railways trains ran with a precision and regularity and even a speed not much improved upon for a hundred years after. They were regulated by "time-tables" which were the first examples of their kind (and occasioned the first use of the word) and their operation relied on the electric telegraph. They were ridden in by men and women who had a few years before only ridden in stagecoaches or carters' wagons. In 1851, a year when a great international exhibition at London advertised her new supremacy, Great Britain smelted two and a half million tons of iron. It does not sound much, but it was five times as much as the United States of America and ten times as much as Germany. At that moment, British steam engines could produce more than 1.2 million horsepower, more than half that of all Europe together.

RATES OF INDUSTRIALIZATION

By 1870 a change had already started to appear in relative positions. Great Britain was still in most ways in the lead, but less decisively, and was not long to remain there. She still had more steam horsepower than any other European country, but the United States (which had already had more in 1850) was ahead of her and Germany was coming up fast. In the 1850s both Germany and France had made the important transition already made in Great Britain from smelting most of their iron by charcoal to smelting with mineral fuels. British superiority in manufacturing iron was still there and her pig-iron output had gone on rising, but now it was only three and a half times that of the United States and four times that of Germany. These were still huge superiorities, none the less, and the age of British industrial dominance had not yet closed.

The industrial countries of which Great Britain was the first were puny creatures in

The mining and building industries, foundries and shipyards grew bigger than ever before and employed large numbers of labourers. This view of a French open-cast mine was painted in 1854.

Sheffield in Yorkshire was Britain's major steel producer. This view of the city dates from c.1885.

comparison with what they were to become. Among them only Great Britain and Belgium had a large majority of their population living in urban districts in the middle of the nineteenth century and the census of 1851 showed that agriculture was still the biggest single employer of labour among British industries (it was rivalled only by domestic service). But in these countries the growing numbers engaged in manufacturing industries, the rise of new concentrations of economic wealth and a new scale of urbanization all made very visible the process of change which was going forward.

URBANIZATION

THIS WAS ESPECIALLY TRUE of the towns. They grew at a spectacular rate in the nineteenth century, particularly in its second half, when the appearance of big centres that would be the nuclei of what a later age would call "conurbations" was especially marked. For the first time, some European cities ceased to depend on rural immigration for their growth. There are difficulties in reckoning indices of urbanization, largely because in different countries urban areas were defined in different ways, but this does not obscure the main lines of what was happening. In 1800 London, Paris and Berlin had, respectively, about 900,000, 600,000 and 170,000 inhabitants. In 1900 the corresponding figures were 4.7 million, 3.6 million and 2.7 million. In that year, too, Glasgow, Moscow, St Petersburg and Vienna also had more than a million inhabitants each. These were the giants; just behind them were sixteen more European cities with over 500,000, a figure passed only by London and Paris in 1800. These great cities and the smaller ones which were still immeasurably bigger than the old ones they overshadowed were still attracting

In late 19th-century Russia, life in the rapidly expanding industrial cities was particularly harsh. For this working-class family, photographed in St Petersburg in the 1890s, home was the rented corner of a room.

immigrants in large numbers from the countryside, notably in Great Britain and Germany. This reflected the tendency for urbanization to be marked in the relatively few countries where industrialization first made headway, because it was the wealth and employment generated by industry which to begin with drew workers to them. Of the twenty-three cities of more than a half-million inhabitants in 1900, thirteen were in four countries, the United Kingdom (six), Germany (three), France (three) and Belgium (one).

LIFE IN THE NEW CITIES

Opinion about cities has undergone many changes. As the eighteenth century ended, something like a sentimental discovery of rural life was in full swing. This coincided with the first phase of industrialization, and the nineteenth century opened with the tide of

aesthetic and moral comment on the turn against a city life which was indeed about to reveal a new and often unpleasant face. That urbanization was seen as an unwelcome, even unhealthy, change by many people, was a tribute to the revolutionary force of what was going on. Conservatives distrusted and feared cities. Long after European governments had demonstrated the ease with which they could control urban unrest, the cities were regarded suspiciously as likely nests of revolution. This is hardly surprising; conditions in many of the new metropolitan centres were often harsh and terrible for the poor. The East End of London could present appalling evidence of poverty, filth, disease and deprivation to anyone who chose to penetrate its slums. A young German businessman, Friedrich Engels, wrote in 1844 one of the most influential books of the century in his study *The Condition of the Working Classes in England* to expose the appalling conditions in which lived the poor of Manchester, and many English-born writers were drawn to similar themes. In France the phenomenon of the "dangerous classes" (as the Parisian poor were called) preoccupied governments for the first half of the century, and misery fired a succession of revolutionary outbreaks between 1789 and 1871. Clearly, it was not unreasonable to fear that the growing cities could breed resentment and hatred of society's rulers and beneficiaries, and that this was a potentially revolutionary force.

THE PLACE OF RELIGION IN THE NEW CITIES

It was also reasonable to predicate that the city made for ideological subversion. It was the great destroyer of traditional patterns of behaviour in nineteenth-century Europe and a crucible of new social forms and ideas, a huge and anonymous thicket in which men and

women easily escaped the scrutiny of priest, squire and neighbours which had been the regulator of rural communities. In it (and this was especially true as literacy slowly spread downwards) new ideas were brought to bear upon long-unchallenged assumptions. Upper-class nineteenth-century Europeans were particularly struck by the seeming tendency of city life to atheism and irreligion. More was at stake, it was felt, than religious truth and sound doctrine (about which the upper classes themselves had long comfortably tolerated disagreement). Religion was the great sustainer of morals and the support of the established social order. A revolutionary writer sneered that religion was "the opium of the people"; the possessing classes would hardly have put it in the same terms, but they acknowledged the importance of religion as social cement. One result was a long-continued series of attempts both in Catholic and Protestant countries to find a way of recapturing the towns for Christianity. The effort was misconceived in so far as it presumed that the Churches had ever had any footing in the urban areas which had long since swamped the traditional parish structures and religious institutions of the old towns and villages at their hearts. But it had a variety of expressions, from the building of new churches in industrial suburbs to the creation of missions combining evangelism and social service which taught churchmen the facts of modern city life. By the end of the century the religious-minded were at least well aware of the challenge they faced, even if their predecessors had not been. One great English evangelist used in the title of one of his books words precisely calculated to emphasize the parallel with missionary work in pagan lands overseas: *Darkest England*. His answer was to found a quite new instrument of religious propaganda, designed to appeal specifically to a new kind of population and to combat

An illustration dated 1881 shows a service held at the Salvation Army headquarters in Whitechapel Road, London. The Salvation Army was founded as an institution for evangelistic and social work by William Booth (1829–1912) in 1878 and quickly spread around the world.

specifically the ills of urban society, the Salvation Army.

THE URBAN POPULATION

The revolution brought by industrialization had an impact far beyond material life. It is an immensely complicated problem to distinguish how modern civilization, the first, so far as we know, which does not have some formal structure of religious belief at its heart, came into being. Perhaps we cannot separate the role of the city in breaking down traditional religious observance from, say, that of science and philosophy in corrupting the belief of the educated. Yet a new future was visible already in the European industrial population of 1870, much of it literate, alienated from traditional authority, secular-

minded and beginning to be conscious of itself as an entity. This was a different basis for civilization from anything yet seen.

THE NEW PACE OF LIFE

To talk of a new basis for civilization is to anticipate, but legitimately, for it suggests once again how rapid and deep was the impact of industrialization on every side of life. Even the rhythm of life changed. For the whole of earlier history, the economic behaviour of most of humanity had been regulated fundamentally by the rhythms of nature. In an agricultural or pastoral economy they imposed a pattern on the year which dictated both the kind of work which had to be undertaken and the kind which could be. Operating within the framework set by the seasons were

From 1840, the number of labourers employed in mines, quarries, steel and iron industries, and machinery and naval industries grew unchecked. Although wages tended to be higher in these industries, fluctuations in demand for products such as those made at this Berlin laminating workshop in 1875 meant that unemployment was a constant threat.

the subordinate divisions of light and darkness, fair weather and foul. People lived in great intimacy with their tools, their animals and the fields in which they won their bread. Even the relatively few town dwellers lived, in large measure, lives shaped by the forces of nature; in Great Britain and France a bad harvest could still blight the whole economy well after 1850. Yet by then many people were already living lives whose rhythms were dictated by quite different pacemakers. Above all they were set by the means of production and their demands – by the need to keep machines economically employed, by the cheapness or dearness of investment capital, by the availability of labour. The symbol of this was the factory whose machinery set a pattern of work in which accurate time-keeping was essential. Men and women began to think in a quite new way about time as a consequence of their industrial work.

As imposing new rhythms, industrialism also related labourers to their work in new ways. It is difficult, but important, to avoid sentimentalizing the past in assessing this. At first sight the disenchantment of the factory worker with his or her monotonous routine, with its exclusion of personal involvement and its background of the sense of working

for another's profit, justifies the rhetoric it has inspired, whether this takes the form of regret for a craftsman's world that has vanished or analysis of what has been identified as the alienation of the worker from the product. But the life of the medieval peasant was monotonous, too, and much of it was spent working for another's profit. Nor is an iron routine necessarily less painful because it is set by sunset and sunrise instead of an employer, or more agreeably varied by drought and tempest than by commercial slump and boom. Yet the new disciplines involved a revolutionary transformation of the ways people won their livelihood, however we may evaluate the results by comparison with what had gone before.

CHILD LABOUR

A CLEAR EXAMPLE of the changes that transformed the workplace can be found in what soon became notorious as one of the persistent evils of early industrialism, its abuse of child labour. An English generation morally braced by the abolition of slavery and by the exaltation that accompanied it was also one intensely aware of the importance of religious training – and therefore of anything which might stand between it and the young – and one disposed to be sentimental about children in a way earlier generations had not been. All this helped to create an awareness of this problem (first, in the United Kingdom) which perhaps distracted attention from the fact that the brutal exploitation of children in factories was only one part of a total transformation of patterns of employment. About the use of children's labour in itself there was nothing new. Children had for centuries provided swineherds, birdscarers, gleaners, maids-of-all-work, crossing-sweepers, prostitutes and

This illustration depicts child workers and their abusive foreman in a London factory in 1848.

casual drudges in Europe (and still do in most non-European societies). The terrible picture of the lot of unprotected children in Hugo's great novel *Les Misérables* (1862) is a picture of their life in a *pre*-industrial society. The difference made by industrialism was that their exploitation was regularized and given a quite new harshness by the institutional forms of the factory. Whereas the work of children in an agricultural society had perforce been clearly differentiated from that of adults by their inferior strength, there existed in the tending of machines a whole range of activity in which children's labour competed directly with that of adults. In a labour market normally over-supplied, this meant that there were irresistible pressures upon the parent to send the child into the factory to earn a contribution to the family income as soon as possible, sometimes at the age of five or six. The consequences were not only often terrible for the victims, but also revolutionary in that the relation of child to society and the structure of the family were blighted. This was one of the "senseless agencies" of history at its most dreadful.

EARLY LEGISLATION

The problems created by industrialization were too pressing to remain without attention and reformers quickly made a start in taming its most obvious evils. By 1850, the law of England had already begun to intervene to protect, for example, women and children in mines and factories; in all the millennia of the history of agriculturally based economies, it had still been impossible by that date to eradicate slavery even in the Atlantic world. Given the unprecedented scale and speed with which social transformation was upon them, the comfortably-off of early industrial Europe need not be blamed without qualification for

The floor in the City of London's New Stock Exchange in 1809 is shown in this engraving taken from a drawing by Thomas Rowlandson.

not acting more quickly to remedy ills whose outlines they could only dimly grasp. Even in the early stage of English industrialism, when, perhaps, the social cost was most heavy, it was difficult to cast off the belief that the liberation of the economy from legal interference was essential to the enormous generation of new wealth which was going on.

ECONOMIC IDEAS

IT IS ALMOST IMPOSSIBLE to find economic theorists and publicists of the early industrial period who advocated absolute non-interference with the economy. Yet there was a broad, sustaining current which favoured the view that much good would result if the market economy was left to operate without the help or hindrance of politicians and civil servants. One force working this way was the teaching often

This mural by William Bell Scott (1811–1890) depicts the docks in Newcastle, northern England, and is dated 1843–1850. It celebrates the region's industrial vigour.

summed up in a phrase made famous by a group of Frenchmen: *laissez-faire*. Broadly speaking, economists after Adam Smith had said with growing consensus that the production of wealth would be accelerated, and therefore the general well-being would increase, if the use of economic resources followed the "natural" demands of the market. Another reinforcing trend was individualism, embodied in both the assumption that individuals knew their own business best and the increasing organization of society around the rights and interests of individuals.

FREE TRADE IN BRITAIN

Individualism and laissez-faire were the sources of the long-enduring association between industrialism and liberalism; they were deplored by conservatives who regretted a hierarchical, agricultural order of mutual obligations and duties, settled ideas, and religious values. Yet liberals who welcomed the new age were by no means taking their stand on a simply negative and selfish base. The creed of "Manchester", as it was called because of the symbolic importance of that city in English industrial and commercial development, was for its leaders much more than a matter of mere self-enrichment. A great political battle which for years preoccupied Englishmen in the early nineteenth century made this clear. Its focus was a campaign for the repeal of what were called the "Corn Laws", a tariff system originally imposed to provide protection for the British farmer from imports of cheaper foreign grain. The "repealers", whose ideological and political leader was a none-too-successful businessman, Richard Cobden, argued that much was at stake. To begin with, retention of the duties on grain demonstrated the grip upon the legislative machinery of the

agricultural interest, the traditional ruling class, who ought not to be allowed a monopoly of power. Opposed to it were the dynamic forces of the future which sought to liberate the national economy from such distortions in the interest of particular groups. Back came the reply of the anti-repealers: the manufacturers were themselves a particular interest who only wanted cheap food imports in order to be able to pay lower wages; if they wanted to help the poor, what about some regulation of the conditions under which they employed women and children in factories? There, the inhumanity of the production process showed a callous disregard for the obligations of privilege which would never have been tolerated in rural England. To this, the repealers responded that cheap food would mean cheaper goods for export. And in this, for someone like Cobden, much more than profit was involved. A worldwide expansion of free trade untrammelled by the

Women working in a British textile mill are shown in an illustration dating from 1851.

interference of mercantilist governments would lead to international progress both material and spiritual, he thought; trade brought peoples together, exchanged and multiplied the blessings of civilization and increased the power in each country of its progressive forces. On one occasion he even committed himself to the view that free trade was the expression of the Divine Will (though even this was not to go as far as the British consul at Canton who had proclaimed that "Jesus Christ is Free Trade, and Free Trade is Jesus Christ").

THE REPEAL OF THE CORN LAWS

There was much more to the free trade issue in Great Britain (of which the Corn Law debate was the focus) than a brief summary can resume. The more it is expounded, the more it becomes clear that industrialism involved creative, positive ideologies which implied intellectual, social and political

challenge to the past. This is why it should not be the subject of simple moral judgments, though both conservatives and liberals thought it could be at the time. The same man might resist legislation to protect the workman against long hours while proving himself a model employer, actively supporting educational and political reform and fighting the corruption of public interest by privileged birth. His opponent might struggle to protect children working in factories and act as a model squire, a benevolent patriarch to his tenants, while bitterly resisting the extension of the franchise to those not members of the established Church or any reduction of the political influence of landlords. It was all very muddled. In the specific issue of the Corn Laws the outcome was paradoxical, too, for a Conservative prime minister was in the end convinced by the arguments of the repealers. When he had the opportunity to do so without too obvious an inconsistency he persuaded Parliament to make the change in 1846. His party contained men who never

This view of Saltaire near Bradford in Yorkshire dates from c.1860. The complex of woollen mills was built on the banks of the Leeds and Liverpool Canal by the English industrialist and Liberal politician Sir Titus Salt (1803–1876). In 1853 he built one of the earliest examples of a model village in the valley for his employees.

forgave him and this great climax of Sir Robert Peel's political career, for which he was to be revered by his Liberal opponents once he was safely out of the way, came shortly before he was dismissed from power by his own followers.

THE BRITISH EXAMPLE AND EUROPEAN OPTIMISM

Only in England was the free trade issue fought out so explicitly and to so clear-cut a conclusion. In other countries, paradoxically, the protectionists soon turned out to have the best of it. Only in the middle of the century, a period of expansion and prosperity, especially for the British economy, did free trade ideas get much support outside the United Kingdom, whose prosperity was regarded by believers as evidence of the correctness of their views and even mollified their opponents; free trade became a British political dogma, untouchable until well into the twentieth century. The prestige of British economic leadership helped to give it a brief popularity elsewhere, too. The prosperity of the era in fact owed as much to other influences as to this ideological triumph, but the belief added to the optimism of economic liberals. Their creed was the culmination of the progressive view of a human being's potential as an individual, whose roots lay in Enlightenment ideas.

The solid grounds for this optimism can nowadays be too easily overlooked. In assessing the impact of industrialism we labour under the handicap of not having before us the squalor of the past it left behind. For all the poverty and the slums (and the very worst was over by then), the people who lived in the great cities of 1900 consumed more and lived longer than their ancestors. This did not, of course, mean they were either tolerably off, by later standards, or contented. But they were often, and probably for the most part, materially better off than their predecessors or most of their contemporaries in the non-European world. Amazing as it may seem, they were part of the privileged minority of mankind. Their longer lives were the best evidence of it.

A poster dated 1886 shows what the completed Eiffel Tower will look like and proclaims that it will be the "main attraction at the Exposition Universelle in Paris in 1889". For many people, the tower symbolized the great optimism and belief in progress that prevailed during this era.

3 POLITICAL CHANGE IN THE AGE OF REVOLUTION

IN THE EIGHTEENTH CENTURY the word "revolution" came to have a new meaning. Traditionally it meant only a change in the composition of government and not necessarily a violent one (though one reason why the English "Glorious Revolution" of 1688 was thought glorious was that it had been non-violent, the English learnt to believe). Observers could speak of a "revolution" occurring at a particular court when one minister replaced another. After 1789 this changed. People came to see that year as the beginning of a new sort of revolution, a real rupture with the past, characterized by violence, by limitless possibilities for fundamental change, social, political and economic, and began to think, too, that this new phenomenon might transcend national boundaries and have something universal and general about it. Even those who disagreed very much about the desirability of such a revolution could none the less agree that this new sort of revolution existed and that it was fundamental to the politics of their age.

British rule in North America

In the 18th century, the subjects of the English colonies in North America enjoyed much more independence and involvement in decision-making than the citizens of most European countries. The colonists could decide on town improvements, hold

public discussions, practise any religion, start up any business and petition their regional assemblies. They were conscious of their dignity, as they saw it, and were accustomed to taking decisions collectively.

The British government, however, made its presence felt. For example, it did not allow the colonies to join together to defend themselves. The British parliament reserved for itself the control of general legal issues, and its intervention from time to time with commerce occasionally caused friction (although this usually stopped short of open conflict).

In the second half of the 18th century, the population, size and wealth of the American colonies were growing rapidly. Problems arose when the British government insisted on keeping a tight rein on territorial, trading, legal and political issues in the face of American demands for greater self-determination. From 1763, a series of restrictive laws was passed, culminating in the 1765 Stamp Act, which was to result in North America's declaration of independence.

King George III of Britain (1738–1820) supported his ministers in their hard-line attitude to the inhabitants of the North American colonies. He considered those who declared independence to be nothing short of rebels.

POLITICS AND REVOLUTION

It would be misleading to seek to group all the political changes of this period under the rubric of "revolution" conceived in such terms as these. But we can usefully speak of an "age of revolution" for two reasons. One is that there were indeed within a century or so many more political upheavals than hitherto which could be called revolutions in this extreme sense, even though many of them failed and others brought results far different from those they had led people to expect. In the second place, if we give the term a little more elasticity, and allow it to cover examples of greatly accelerated and fundamental political change which certainly go beyond the replacement of one set of governors by another, then there are many less dramatic political changes in these years which are distinctly revolutionary in their effect. The first and most obvious was the dissolution of the first British empire, whose central episode later became known as the American Revolution.

BRITISH COLONIES IN NORTH AMERICA

In 1763 BRITISH IMPERIAL POWER in North America was at its height. Canada had been taken from the French; the old fear of a Mississippi valley cordon of French forts enclosing the thirteen colonies had been blown away. This might seem to dispose of

any grounds for future misgiving, yet some prophets had already suggested, even before the French defeat, that their removal might not strengthen but weaken the British grasp on North America. In the British colonies, after all, there were already more colonists then there were subjects in many sovereign states of Europe. Many were neither of English descent nor native English-speakers. They had economic interests not necessarily congruent with those of the imperial power. Yet the grip of the British government on them was bound to be slack, simply because of the huge distances which separated London from the colonies. Once the threat from the French (and from the Native North Americans whom the French had egged on) was gone, the ties of empire might have to be allowed to grow slacker still.

This 18th-century woodcut depicts slaves supposedly greeting a wealthy plantation owner and his family in the state of Virginia.

Time chart (1765–1814)					
		1774 First Continental Congress in Philadelphia	1783 End of the War of Independence	1803 The Louisiana Purchase	
	1767 Townshend Acts				
1750				1800	
1765 Stamp Act	1773 Boston Tea Party	1775 Outbreak of the War of Independence	1787 Constitution of the United States of America	1812–14 War against Great Britain and Canada	

THE POTENTIAL FOR AMERICAN INDEPENDENCE

Difficulties appeared almost at once in the wake of the French expulsion. How was the West to be organized? What relation was it to have to the existing colonies? How were the new Canadian subjects of the Crown to be treated? These problems were given urgency by "Pontiac's rebellion", a Native North American revolt in the Ohio valley in 1763 in response to pressure by the colonists who saw the West as their proper domain for settlement and trade. The imperial government immediately proclaimed the area west of the Alleghenies closed to settlement. This, as a start, offended many colonials who had looked forward to the exploitation of these regions, and it was followed by still more irritation as British administrators negotiated treaties with Native North Americans and worked out arrangements for a garrisoned frontier to protect the colonists and Native North Americans from one another.

Ten years followed during which the dormant potential for American independence matured and came to a head. Grumbles about grievances turned first into resistance, then rebellion. Time after time, colonial politicians used provocative British legislation to radicalize American politics by making the colonists believe that the practical liberty they already enjoyed was in danger. The pace throughout was set by British initiatives. Paradoxically, Great Britain was ruled at this time by a succession of ministers anxious to carry out reforms in colonial affairs; their excellent intentions helped to destroy a status quo which had previously proved workable. They thus provide one of the first examples of what was to be a frequent phenomenon of the next few decades, the goading of vested interests into rebellion by well-meant but politically ill-judged reform.

TAXATION OF THE COLONIES

One principle firmly grasped in London was that the Americans ought to pay a proper share of the taxes which contributed to their defence and the common good of the empire. There were two distinct attempts to assure this. The first, in 1764–5, took the form of imposing duties on sugar imported to the colonies and a Stamp Act which was to raise money from revenue stamps to be put on various classes of legal documents. The important thing about these was not the amounts they proposed to raise nor even the novelty of taxing the internal transactions of the colonies (which was much discussed) but rather that these were, as both British politicians and American taxpayers saw, unilateral acts of legislation by the imperial parliament. The usual way in which colonial affairs were handled and revenue raised hitherto had been by haggling with their own assemblies. What was now brought into question was some-

Benjamin Franklin (1706–1790), philosopher, physicist and North American statesman, was commissioned to take the American protest against the Stamp Act to London. When the British government rejected his demands, Franklin, who had previously believed that it was possible for America to develop freely within the British Empire, returned to North America in 1775 to take an active part in the debate that would lead to the Declaration of Independence the following year.

thing so far hardly even formulated as a question: whether the undoubted legislative sovereignty of the parliament of the United Kingdom also extended to its colonies. Riots, non-importation agreements and angry protest followed. The unhappy officials who held the stamps were given a bad time. Ominously, representatives of nine colonies attended a Stamp Act Congress to protest. The Stamp Act was withdrawn.

The London government then took a different tack in its second fiscal initiative. It turned to external duties on paint, paper, glass and tea. As these were not internal taxes and the imperial government had always regulated trade, they seemed more promising. But it proved an illusion. Americans were by now being told by their radical politicians that no taxation at all should be levied on them by a legislature in which they were not represented. As George III saw, it was not the Crown but Parliament whose power was under attack. There were more riots and boycotts and one of the first of those influential scuffles which make up so much of the history of decolonization, when the death of possibly five rioters in 1770 was mythologized into a "Boston Massacre".

RADICAL COLONIAL POLITICIANS

Once more, the British government retreated. Three of the duties were withdrawn: that on tea remained. Unfortunately, the issue was by now out of hand; it transcended taxation, as the British government saw, and had become one of whether or not the imperial parliament could make laws enforceable in the colonies. As George III put it a little later: "We must either master them, or totally leave them to themselves." The issue was focused in one place, though it manifested itself throughout the colonies. By 1773, after the destruction of

a cargo of tea by radicals (the "Boston Tea Party"), the crucial question for the British government was: could Massachusetts be governed?

There were to be no more retreats: George III, his ministers and the majority of the House of Commons were agreed on this. A number of coercive acts were passed to bring Boston to heel. The New England radicals were heard all the more sympathetically in the other colonies at this juncture because a humane and sensible measure providing for the future of Canada, the Quebec Act of 1774 stirred up wide feeling. Some disliked the privileged position it gave to Roman Catholicism (it was intended to leave French Canadians as undisturbed as possible in their ways by their change of rulers), while others saw its extension of Canadian boundaries south to the Ohio as another block to expansion in the west. In September the same year there met a Continental Congress of delegates from the colonies at Philadelphia. It severed

A contemporary engraving depicts the Boston Massacre of 5 March, 1770 – the first recorded violent incident of the American Revolution – in which five people were killed. Of the nine British soldiers later tried for murder, seven were acquitted and two found guilty of manslaughter.

The boycott against the British tariffs increased and the general unrest in the North American colonies began to be channelled through committees. The women of Edenton, North Carolina, who are represented in this 18th-century engraving, swore not to drink any more tea until their country gained its freedom.

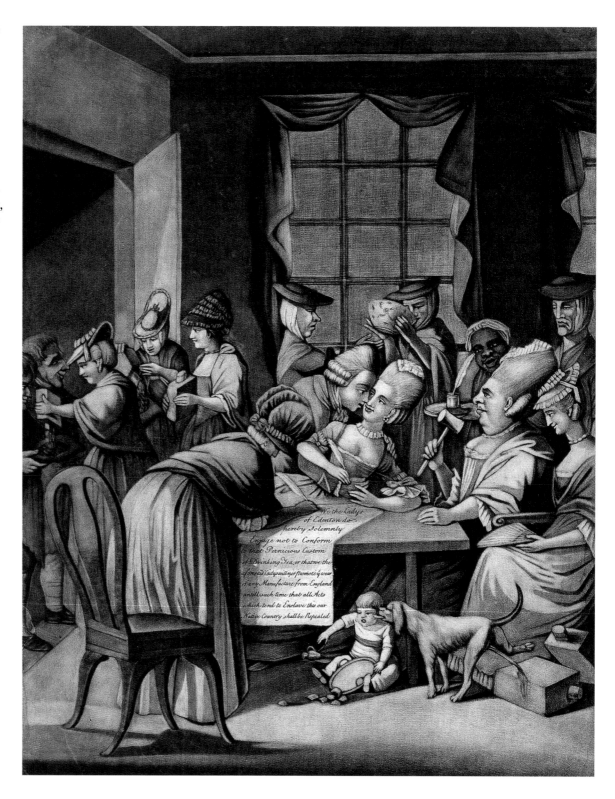

commercial relations with the United Kingdom and demanded the repeal of much existing legislation, including the Quebec Act. By this time the recourse to force was probably inevitable. The radical colonial politicians had brought out into the open the practical sense of independence already felt by many Americans. But it was inconceivable that any eighteenth-century imperial government could have grasped this. The British government was in fact remarkably reluctant to act on its convictions by relying simply on force until disorder and intimidation of the law-abiding and moderate colonials had already gone very far. At the same time, it made it clear that it would not willingly bend on the principles of sovereignty.

THE DECLARATION OF INDEPENDENCE

Arms were gathered in Massachusetts. In April 1775 a detachment of British soldiers sent to Lexington to seize some of them fought the first action of the American Revolution. It was not quite the end of the beginning. It took a year more for the feelings of the colonists' leaders to harden into the conviction that only complete independence from Great Britain would rally an effective resistance. The result was the Declaration of Independence of July 1776, and the debate was transferred to the battlefield.

This engraving, dated 1774, depicts the first pan-colonial congress, at Philadelphia, which was attended by delegates from the 13 colonies. They agreed to suspend trade with Britain until the rights that the colonies had enjoyed prior to 1763 were re-established and all legislation since that date rescinded. Resolutions were also passed to pay no taxes to Britain, and to prepare to defend the colonies if British troops attacked them.

The American Declaration of Independence, 4 July, 1776

"We hold these truths to be self-evident: that all men are created equal, that they are endowed by their Creator with certain unalienable Rights, that among these are Life, Liberty, and the pursuit of Happiness. That to secure these rights, Governments are instituted among Men, deriving their just powers from the consent of the governed.

"That whenever any Form of Government becomes destructive of these ends, it is the Right of the People to alter or to abolish it, and to institute new Government, laying its foundation on such principles and organizing its powers in such form, as to them shall seem most likely to effect their Safety and Happiness.

"The history of the present King of Great Britain is a history of repeated injuries and usurpations, all having in direct object the establishment of an absolute Tyranny over these States. ...

"We, therefore, the Representatives of the United States of America ... do ... solemnly publish and declare, That these United Colonies are, and of Right ought to be Free and Independent States; that they are Absolved from all Allegiance to the British Crown, and that all political connection between them and the State of Great Britain, is ... totally dissolved; and that as Free and Independent States, they have full Power to levy War, conclude Peace, contract Alliances, establish Commerce, and to do all other Acts ... which Independent States may of right do. And for the support of this Declaration ..., we mutually pledge to each other our Lives, our Fortunes and our ... Honor."

An extract from the Declaration of Independence.

The first armed conflict of the American War of Independence took place on 18 April, 1775. This engraving depicts the surrender of Britain's General Burgoyne to the American leader General Gates at Saratoga Springs on 17 October, 1777.

British arms and the end of an era of imperial rule. Peace negotiations soon began and two years later, at Paris, a treaty was signed in which Great Britain recognized the independence of the United States of America, whose territory the British negotiators had already conceded should run to the Mississippi. This was a crucial decision in the shaping of a new nation; the French, who had envisaged making a recovery in the Mississippi valley, were disappointed. The northern continent was to be shared by the rebels only with Spain and Great Britain, it appeared.

The British lost the war which followed because of the difficulties imposed by geography, because American generalship succeeded in avoiding superior forces long enough to preserve an army which could impose its will on them at Saratoga in 1777, because the French entered the war soon afterwards to win a return match for the defeat of 1763, and because the Spanish followed them and thus tipped the balance of naval power. The British had a further handicap; they dared not fight the kind of war which might win military victory by terrorizing the American population and thus encouraging those who wished to remain under the British flag to cut off the supplies and freedom of movement which General Washington's army enjoyed. They could not do this because their over-riding aim had to be to keep open the way to a conciliatory peace with colonists willing again to accept British rule. In these circumstances, the Bourbon coalition was fatal. The military decision came in 1781, when a British army found itself trapped at Yorktown between the Americans on land and a French squadron at sea. Only seven thousand or so men were involved, but their surrender was the worst humiliation yet undergone by

A NEW NATION

FOR ALL THE LOOSE ENDS which would need to be tied up, and a number of boundary disputes which dragged on for decades to come, the appearance of a new state of great potential resources in the western hemisphere was by any standard certainly a revolutionary change. If it was at first often seen as something less than this by foreign observers, that was because the weaknesses of the new nation were at the time more apparent than its potential. Indeed, it was far from clear that it was a nation at all; the colonies were weak and divided and many expected them to fall to quarrelling and disunion. Their great and inestimable advantage was their remoteness. They could work out their problems virtually untroubled by foreign intervention, a blessing crucial to much that was to follow.

Victory in war was followed by a half-dozen critical years during which a handful of American politicians took decisions which were to shape much of the future history of the world. As in all civil wars and wars of independence, deep divisions had been created which accentuated political weakness. Among these, those which divided loyalists from rebels were, for all their bitterness,

General George Washington (1732–1799), who was designated commander-in-chief of the American forces, had to face the British troops, the Americans who remained loyal to the British and the warriors of the Native American tribes who had allied themselves with the colonists' enemy. Washington later became the first president of the United States.

John Paul Jones (a naval officer), Benjamin Franklin and George Washington enter Independence Hall, Philadelphia, during the Constitutional Convention of 1787.

perhaps the least important. That problem had been solved, brutally, by emigration of the defeated; something like 80,000 loyalists left the rebel colonies, for a variety of motives running from dislike of intimidation and terror to simple loyalty to the Crown. Other divisions were likely to cause more trouble in the future. Class and economic interests separated farmers, merchants and plantation-owners. There were important differences between the new states which had replaced the former colonies and between the regions or sections of a rapidly developing country; one of these, that imposed by the economic importance of black slavery to the southern states, was to take decades to work out. On the other hand, the Americans also had great advantages as they set about nation-building. They faced the future without the terrible incubus of a huge illiterate and backward peasant population such as stood in the way of evolving a democratic system in many other countries. They had ample territory and great economic resources even in their existing areas of occupation (though the extent of these could not yet be known). Finally, they had European civilization to draw upon, subject only to the modifications its legacies might undergo in transplantation to a virgin – or near-virgin – continent.

THE AMERICAN CONSTITUTION

The war against the British had imposed a certain discipline. Articles of Confederation had been agreed between the former colonies and came into force in 1781. In them appeared the name of the new nation, the United States of America. The peace brought a growing sense that these arrangements were unsatisfactory. There were two areas of particular concern. One was disturbance arising fundamentally from disagreement about what the Revolution ought to have meant in domestic affairs. The central government came to many Americans to appear to be far too weak to deal with disaffection and disorder. The other arose from a post-war economic depression, particularly affecting external trade and linked to currency problems arising from the independence of individual states. To deal with these, too, the central government seemed ill-equipped. It

was accused of neglecting American economic interests in its conduct of relations with other countries. Whether true or not, this was widely believed. The outcome was a meeting of delegates from the states in a constitutional convention at Philadelphia in 1787. After four months' work they signed a draft constitution which was then submitted to the individual states for ratification. When nine states had ratified it the constitution came into effect in the summer of 1788. In April 1789 George Washington, the former commander of the American forces in the war against the British, took the oath of office as the first president of the new republic, thus inaugurating a series of presidencies which has continued unbroken to this day.

Much was said about the need for simple institutions and principles clear in their intention, yet the new constitution was still to be revealing its potential for development two hundred years later. For all the determination of its drafters to provide a document which would unambiguously resist reinterpretation, they were (fortunately) unsuccessful. The United States constitution was to prove capable of spanning a historical epoch which turned a scatter of largely agricultural

This portrayal of the signing of the constitution of the United States in 1787 was painted in 1940 by Howard Chandler Christy for the Hall of Representatives in Washington, DC.

societies into a giant and industrial world power. In part this was because of the provision for conscious amendment, but in larger measure it was due to the evolving interpretation of the doctrines it embodied. But also much remained unchanged; though often formal, these features of the constitution are very important. Besides them, too, there were fundamental principles which were to endure, even if there was much argument about what they might mean.

REPUBLICANISM

To begin with the most obvious fact: the constitution was republican. This was by no means normal in the eighteenth century and should not be taken for granted. Some Americans felt that republicanism was so important and so insecure that they even disapproved of the constitution because they thought it (and particularly its installation of a president as the head of the executive)

"squinted towards monarchy", as one of them put it. The ancient republics were as familiar to classically educated Europeans for their tendency to decay and faction as for their legendarily admirable morals. The history of the Italian republics was unpromising, too, and much more unedifying than that of Athens and Rome. Republics in eighteenth-century Europe were few and apparently unflourishing. They seemed to persist only in small states, though it was conceded that the remoteness of the United States might protect republican forms which would elsewhere ensure the collapse of a large state. Still, observers were not sanguine about the new nation. The later success of the United States was therefore to be of incalculable importance in reversing opinion about republicanism. Very soon, its capacity to survive, its cheapness and a liberalism wrongly thought to be inseparable from it focused the attention of critics of traditional governments all over the civilized world. European advocates of political change soon began to

The inauguration of President George Washington, depicted here, took place in New York's Old City Hall on 30 April, 1789. Washington went on to be re-elected as president in 1793 and remained in office until 1797.

The centre of American political life was to be the Capitol, pictured here towards the final stages of its construction. George Washington, who laid its first stone in 1792, also participated in the planning of the federal capital city that bears his name. Congress moved into the Capitol building in Washington, DC in 1800.

look to America for inspiration; soon, too, the influence of republican example was to spread from the northern to the southern American continent.

THE BRITISH INFLUENCE

The second characteristic of the new constitution which was of fundamental importance was that its roots lay largely in British political experience. Besides the law of England, whose Common Law principles passed into the jurisprudence of the new state, this was true also of the actual arrangement of government. The founding fathers had all grown up in the British colonial system in which elected assemblies had debated the public interest with monarchical governors. They instituted a bicameral legislature (although they excluded any hereditary element in its composition) on the English model, to offset a president. They thus followed English constitutional theory in putting a monarch, albeit an elected one, at the head of the executive machinery of government. This was not how the British constitution of the eighteenth century actually worked, but it was a good approximation to its theory. What they did, in fact, was to take the best constitution they knew, purge it of its corruptions (as they saw them) and add to it the modifications appropriate to American political and social circumstance. What they did not do was to emulate the alternative principle of government available in contemporary Europe, monarchical absolutism, even in its enlightened form. The Americans wrote a constitution for free citizens because they believed that the British already lived under one. They thought it had failed only in so far as it had been corrupted, and that it had been improperly employed to deprive Americans of the rights they too ought to have possessed under it. Because of this, the same principles of government (albeit in much evolved forms)

The bustling streets of New York City are depicted on the morning of Inauguration Day, 1789.

of the central government and the individual states. It was a debate which would in the end come within an ace of destroying the Union. Federalism would also promote a major re-adjustment within the constitution, the rise of the Supreme Court as an instrument of judi-cial review. Outside the Union, the nineteenth century would reveal the appeal of federalism to many other countries, impressed by what appeared to have been achieved by the Americans. Federalism was to be seen by European liberals as a crucial device for reconciling unity with freedom and British governments found it a great standby in their handling of colonial problems.

would one day be propagated and patronized in areas which shared none of the cultural assumptions of the Anglo-Saxon world on which they rested.

FEDERALISM

One way in which the United States differed radically from most other existing states and diverged consciously from the British constitutional model was in adherence to the principle of federalism. This was indeed fun-damental to it, since only large concessions to the independence of individual states made it possible for the new union to come into exis-tence at all. The former colonies had no wish to set up a new central government which would bully them as they believed the govern-ment of King George had done. The federal structure provided an answer to the problem of diversity – *e pluribus unum*. It also dictated much of the form and content of American politics for the next eighty years. Question after question whose substance was economic or social or ideological would find itself pressed into the channels of a continuing debate about what were the proper relations

DEMOCRACY

Finally, in any summary, however brief, of the historic significance of the constitution of the United States, attention must be given to its opening words: "We the People" (even though they seem to have been included almost casually). The actual political arrange-ments in several of the states of 1789 were by no means democratic, but the principle of popular sovereignty was enunciated clearly from the start. In whatever form the mythol-ogy of a particular historical epoch might cloak it, the popular will was to remain the ultimate court of appeal in politics for Americans. Here was a fundamental depar-ture from British constitutional practice, and it owed something to the way in which seven-teenth-century colonists had sometimes given themselves constitutions. Yet this had been within the overall framework of kingship. British constitutionalism was prescriptive; the sovereignty of king in parliament was not there because the people had once decided it should be, but because it was there and was unquestioned. As the great English constitutional historian Maitland once put it,

Englishmen had taken the authority of the Crown as a substitute for the theory of the state. The new constitution broke with this and with every other prescriptive theory (though this was not quite a clean break with British political thinking, for Locke had said in the 1680s that governments held their powers on trust and that the people could upset governments which abused that trust, and on this ground, among others, some Englishmen had justified the Glorious Revolution).

The American adoption of a democratic theory that all governments derive their just powers from the consent of the governed, as it had been put as early as the Declaration of Independence, was epoch-marking. But it by no means solved the problems of political authority at a stroke. Many Americans feared what a democracy might do and sought to restrict the popular element in the political system right from the start. Another problem was suggested by the fundamental rights set out in the first ten amendments to the constitution at the end of 1789. These were presumably as much open to reamendment at the hands of popular sovereignty as any other part of the constitution. Here was an important source of disagreement for the future: Americans have always found it easy to be somewhat confused (especially in the affairs of other countries but even in their own at times) about whether democratic principles consist in following the wishes of the majority or in upholding certain fundamental rights. Nevertheless, the adoption of the democratic principle in 1787 was immensely important and justifies the consideration of the constitution as a landmark in world history. For generations to come the new United States would become the focus of the aspirations of those longing to be free the world over – "the world's last, best hope", as one American once said. Even today, when America has become a great conservative nation, the democratic ideal of which for so long it was the custodian and exemplar retains its power in many countries, and the institutions it fertilized are still working.

FRANCE IN THE REVOLUTIONARY ERA

PARIS WAS THE CENTRE of social and political discussion in Europe. To it returned some of the French soldiers who had helped to bring to birth the young American Republic. It is hardly surprising, then, that although most European nations in some measure responded to the transatlantic revolution, the French were especially aware of it. American example and the hopes it raised were a contribution, though a subsidiary one, to the huge release of forces which is still, in spite of later upheavals, called *the* French Revolution. Unfortunately, this all too familiar and simple term puts

This anti-royalist caricature from the era of the French Revolution is entitled *La Chasse aux Aristocrates*. The imagery of this turbulent period abounds with depictions of nobles and clerics being hounded and ridiculed by revolutionaries.

The ill-fated King Louis XVI (1754–1793) reigned to see the French monarchy replaced by a republic.

obstacles in the way of understanding. Politicians and scholars have offered many different interpretations of what the essence of the Revolution was, have disagreed about how long it went on and what were its results, and even about when it began. They agree about little except that what began in 1789 was very important. Within a very short time, indeed, it changed the whole concept of revolution, though there was much in it that

The Swiss-born banker Jacques Necker (1732–1804) was director-general of French finance from 1777. His reform programmes incurred the queen's wrath and resulted in his dismissal in 1781. Necker was recalled to office in 1788, and recommended the summoning of the Estates General.

looked to the past rather than the future. It was a great boiling-over of the pot of French society and the pot's contents were a jumbled mixture of conservative and innovating elements much like those of the 1640s in England, and equally confused in their mixture of consciousness and unconsciousness of direction and purposes, too.

FINANCIAL PROBLEMS

Confusion was the symptom of big dislocations and maladjustments in the material life and government of France. She was the greatest of European powers and her rulers neither could nor wished to relinquish her international role. The first way in which the American Revolution had affected her was by providing an opportunity for revenge; Yorktown was the retaliation for defeat at the hands of the British in the Seven Years' War, and to deprive them of the Thirteen Colonies was some compensation for the French loss of India and Canada. Yet the successful effort was costly. The second great consequence was

that for no considerable gain beyond the humiliation of a rival, France added yet another layer to the huge and accumulating debt piled up by her efforts since the 1630s to build and maintain her European supremacy.

Attempts to liquidate this debt and cut the monarchy free from the cramping burden it imposed (and it was becoming clear after 1783 that France's real independence in foreign affairs was narrowing sharply because of it) were made by a succession of ministers under Louis XVI, the young, somewhat stupid, but high-principled and well-meaning king who came to the throne in 1774. None of them succeeded in even arresting the growth of the debt, let alone in reducing it. What was worse, their effects only advertised the facts of failure. The deficit could be measured and the figures published as would never have been possible under Louis XIV. If there was a spectre haunting France in the 1780s, it was not that of revolution but of state bankruptcy.

The essential problem was that the whole social and political structure of France stood in the way of tapping the wealth of the better-off, the only sure way of emerging from the financial impasse. Ever since the days of Louis XIV himself, it had proved impossible to levy a due weight of taxation on the wealthy without resorting to force, for the whole legal and social structure of France, its

Time chart (1789–1815)

		1791 Constitution Legislative Assembly		1804 Napoleon becomes Emperor		1814 Paris Peace Treaty Louis XVIII King of France	
1750						1850	
	1789 National Assembly		1792 The National Convention declares the Republic		1799 The Consulate	1815 Battle of Waterloo Napoleon banished to St Helena	

privileges, special immunities and prescriptive rights, blocked the way ahead. The paradox of eighteenth-century government was at its most evident in France; a theoretically absolute monarchy could not infringe the mass of liberties and rights which made up the essentially medieval constitution of the country without threatening its own foundations. Monarchy itself rested on prescription.

POLARIZATION

To more and more Frenchmen it appeared that France needed a transformation of her governmental and constitutional structure if she was to emerge from her difficulties. But some went further. They saw in the inability of government to share fiscal burdens equitably between classes the extreme example of a whole range of abuses which needed reform. The issue was more and more exaggerated in terms of polarities: of reason and superstition, of freedom and slavery, of humanitarianism and greed. Above all, it tended to concentrate on the symbolic question of legal privilege. The class which focused the anger this aroused was the nobility, an immensely diverse and very large body (there seem to have been between 200,000 and 250,000 noble males in France in 1789) about which cultural, economic or social generalization is impossible, but whose members all shared a legal status which in some degree conferred privilege at law.

THE ESTATES GENERAL MEETS

While the logic of financial extremity pushed the governments of France more and more towards conflict with the privileged, there was a natural unwillingness on the part of many of the royal advisers, themselves usually noblemen, and of the king himself to proceed except by agreement. When in 1788 a series of failures nerved the government to accept that conflict was inevitable, it still sought to

An engraving after an original contemporary drawing by a court painter shows the opening of the Estates General meeting in Versailles on 5 May, 1789.

confine the conflict to legal channels, and, like Englishmen in 1640, turned to historic institutions for means to do so. Not having Parliament to hand, they trundled out from the attic of French constitutionalism the nearest thing to a national representative body that France had ever possessed, the Estates General. This body of representatives of nobles, clergy and commoners had not met since 1614. It was hoped that it would provide sufficient moral authority to squeeze agreement from the fiscally privileged for the payment of higher taxes. It was an unimpeachably constitutional step, but as a solution had the disadvantage that great expectations were aroused while what the Estates General could legally do was obscure. More than one answer was given. Some already said the Estates General could legislate for the nation, even if historic and undoubted legal privileges were at issue.

SOCIAL STRAINS

This very complicated political crisis was coming to a head at the end of a period in which France was also under other strains. Underlying everything was an increasing population. Since the second quarter of the century this had risen at what a later age would think a slow rate, but still fast enough to outstrip growth in the production of food. This sustained a long-run inflation of food prices which bore most painfully upon the poor, the vast majority of the French who were peasants with little or no land. Given the coincidence of the fiscal demands of governments – which for a long time staved off the financial crisis by borrowing or by putting up the direct and indirect taxes which fell most heavily on the poor – and the efforts of landlords to protect themselves in inflationary times by holding down wages and putting up

rents and dues, the life of the poor in France was growing harsher and more miserable for nearly all the century. To this general impoverishment should be added the special troubles which from time to time afflicted particular regions or classes, but which, coincidentally, underwent something of an intensification in the second half of the 1780s. Bad harvests, cattle disease, and recession, which badly affected the areas where peasants' families produced textiles as a supplement to their income, all sapped the precarious health of the economy in the 1780s. The sum effect was that the elections to the Estates General in 1789 took place in a very excited and embittered atmosphere.

Entitled *The Village Man, Born into Hard Labour*, this 18th-century French engraving aims to show the harsh conditions in which peasants worked and bemoans the fact that most of their meagre incomes went to rent and tax collectors.

Millions of French people were desperately seeking some way out of their troubles, were eager to seek and blame scapegoats, and had quite unrealistic and inflated notions of what good the king, whom they trusted, could do for them.

Thus a complex interplay of governmental impotence, social injustice, economic hardship and reforming aspiration brought about the French Revolution. But before this complexity is lost to sight in the subsequent political battles and the simplifying slogans they generated, it is important to emphasize that almost no one either anticipated this outcome or desired it. There was much social injustice in France, but no more than many other eighteenth-century states found it possible to live with. There was a welter of expectant and hopeful advocates of particular reforms ranging from the abolition of the censorship to the prohibition of immoral and irreligious literature, but no one doubted that such changes could easily be carried out by the king, once he was informed of his people's wishes and needs. What did not exist was a party of revolution clearly confronting a party of reaction.

THE REVOLUTIONARY DECADE

Parties only came into existence when the Estates General had met. This is one reason why the day on which they did so, 5 May, 1789 (a week after George Washington's inauguration), is a date in world history, because it opened an era in which to be for or against the Revolution became the central political question in most continental countries, and even tainted the very different politics of Great Britain and the United States. What happened in France was bound to matter elsewhere. At the simplest level this was because she was the greatest European

On 20 June, 1789, the new National Assembly met in the tennis court at Versailles (having been barred from their usual meeting place), and swore "never to part again ... until the constitution of the kingdom is established on firm foundations". The Tennis Court Oath, as this event became known, is depicted in this illustration by Jacques-Louis David (1748–1825), dated 1791.

By the middle of the summer of 1789, popular hostility towards the Crown was rife and rumours that the king's troops had been ordered to storm the capital were circulating. Unrest broke out on the streets of Paris during the night of 12–13 July, as portrayed in this illustration, and culminated in the storming of the Bastille on 14 July.

power; the Estates General would either paralyse her (as many foreign diplomats hoped) or liberate her from her difficulties to play again a forceful role. Beyond this, France was also the cultural leader of Europe. What her writers and politicians said and did was immediately accessible to people elsewhere because of the universality of the French language, and it was bound to be given respectful attention because people were in the habit of looking to Paris for intellectual guidance.

THE NEW NATIONAL ASSEMBLY

In the summer of 1789 the Estates General turned itself into a national assembly claiming sovereignty. Breaking with the assumption that it represented the great medieval divisions of society, the majority of its members claimed to represent all Frenchmen without distinction. It was able to take this

revolutionary step because the turbulence of France frightened the government and those deputies to the assembly who opposed such a change. Rural revolt and Parisian riot alarmed ministers no longer sure that they could rely upon the army. This led first to the monarchy's abandonment of the privileged classes, and then to its concession, unwillingly and uneasily, of many other things asked for by the politicians who led the new National Assembly. At the same time these concessions created a fairly clear-cut division between those who were for the Revolution and those who were against it; in language to go round the world they were soon called Left and Right (because of the places in which they sat in the assembly).

The main task which the National Assembly set itself was the writing of a constitution, but in the process it transformed the whole institutional structure of France. Before 1791, when it dispersed, it had nationalized the lands of the Church,

On the night of 4 August, 1789, the National Assembly abolished feudal rights in the meeting depicted. On 26 August, the Declaration of the Rights of Man and of the Citizen received the Assembly's approval.

On 14 July, 1789, the people of Paris stormed the state prison, the Bastille, as this engraving shows. Lafayette took charge of the newly created National Guard. In the provinces the peasants revolted and revolutionary town councils were created.

abolished what it termed "the feudal system", ended censorship, created a system of central-ized representative government, obliterated the old provincial and local divisions and replaced them with the "departments" under which the French still live, instituted equality before the law, and separated the exec-utive from the legislative power. These were only the most remarkable things done by one of the most remarkable parliamentary bodies the world has ever seen. Its failures tend to mask this huge achievement; they should not be allowed to do so. Broadly speaking, they removed the legal and institutional checks on the modernization of France. Popular sov-ereignty, administrative centralization, and individual legal equality were from this time poles towards which her institutional life always returned.

Many in France did not like all this; some liked none of it. By 1791 the king had given clear evidence of his own misgivings, the goodwill which had supported him in the early Revolution was gone and he was

In 1791, strikes were organized in Parisian cafés such as this one on the Boulevard du Temple.

Maximilien de Robespierre (1758–1794), deputy in the Estates General for the commoners, represented the extreme left in his democratic convictions and became a leader of the radical Jacobins. Elected to the ruling Committee for Public Safety in 1793, he lost its support the following year when fellow committee members sent him to the guillotine for his role in the Terror.

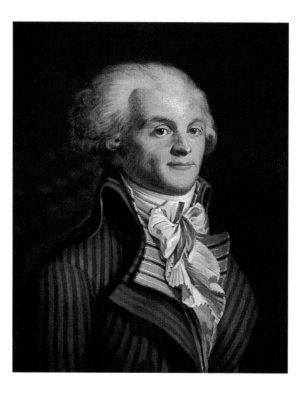

The Rights of Man and of the Citizen

1. Men are born and remain free and equal in rights; social distinctions may be based only upon general usefulness.
2. The aim of every political association is the preservation of the natural and inalienable rights of man; these rights are liberty, property, security, and resistance to oppression.
3. The source of all sovereignty resides essentially in the nation; no group, no individual may exercise authority not emanating expressly therefrom. ...
9. Since every man is presumed innocent until declared guilty ... all unnecessary severity for securing the person of the accused must be severely repressed by law.
10. No one is to be disquieted because of his opinions, even religious, provided their manifestation does not disturb the public order established by law.
11. Free communication of ideas and opinions is one of the most precious of the rights of man. Consequently, every citizen may speak, write, and print freely, subject to responsibility for the abuse of such liberty in the cases determined by law. ...
16. Every society in which the guarantee of rights is not assured or the separation of powers not determined has no constitution at all.

Extracts from the Declaration of the Rights of Man and of the Citizen, as published by the National Assembly on 27 August, 1789.

suspected as an anti-revolutionary. Some noblemen had already disliked enough of what was going on to emigrate; they were led by two of the king's brothers, which did not improve the outlook for royalty. But most important of all, many of the French turned against the Revolution when, because of papal policy, the National Assembly's settlement of Church affairs was called in question. Much in it had appealed deeply to many in France, churchmen among them, but the pope rejected it and this raised the ultimate question of authority. French Catholics had to decide whether the authority of the pope or that of the French constitution was supreme for them. This created the most important division which came to embitter revolutionary politics.

THE END OF THE FRENCH MONARCHY

In 1792 a great crisis occurred. France went to war with Austria at the beginning of the year and with Prussia soon after. The issue was complicated but many French people believed that foreign powers wished to intervene to bring the Revolution to an end and put the clock back to 1788. By the summer, as things went badly and shortages and suspicion mounted at home, the king was discredited. A Parisian insurrection overthrew the monarchy and led to the summoning of a new assembly to draw up a new and, this time, republican constitution. This body,

Popular demonstrations on 10 August, 1792 in Paris convinced Robespierre that the only legality was that of the people. These revolutionary-era drawings represent Parisian *sans-culottes*, so called because the men wore long trousers rather than the knee breeches of the nobility under the old régime.

called the Convention, was the centre of French government until 1796. Through civil and foreign war and economic and ideological crisis it achieved the survival of the Revolution. Most of its members were politically not much more advanced in their views than their predecessors. They believed in the individual and the sanctity of property (they prescribed the death penalty for anyone proposing a law to introduce agrarian communism) and that the poor are always with us, though they allowed some of them a small say in affairs by supporting direct universal adult male suffrage. What distinguished them from their predecessors was that they were willing to go rather further to meet emergencies than earlier French assemblies (especially when frightened by the possibility of defeat); they sat in a capital city which was for a long time manipulated by more extreme politicians to push them into measures more radical than they really wanted, and into using very democratic language. Consequently, they frightened Europe much more than their predecessors had done.

THE TERROR

The Convention's symbolic break with the past came when it voted for the execution of the king in January 1793. The judicial murder of kings had hitherto been believed to be an English aberration; now the English were as shocked as the rest of Europe. They, too, now went to war with France, because they feared the strategical and commercial result of French success against the Austrians in the Netherlands. But the war looked more and more like an ideological struggle and to win it the French government appeared increasingly bloodthirsty at home. A new instrument for

The reign of Louis XVI ended in September 1792 when a republic was proclaimed, ruled by a National Convention. Its Jacobin wing accused the king of conspiring to overthrow the republic and he was narrowly found guilty of treason. His execution took place on 21 January, 1793.

humane execution, the guillotine (a characteristic product of pre-revolutionary enlightenment, combining as it did technical efficiency and benevolence in the swift, sure death it afforded its victims), became the symbol of the Terror, the name soon given to a period during which the Convention strove by intimidation of its enemies at home to assure survival to the Revolution. There was much that was misleading in this symbolism. Some of the Terror was only rhetoric, the hot air of politicians trying to keep up their own spirits and frighten their opponents. In practice it often reflected a jumble of patriotism, practical necessity, muddled idealism, self-interest and petty vengefulness, as old scores were settled in the name of the republic. Many people died, of course – something over 35,000, perhaps – and many emigrated to avoid danger, yet the guillotine killed only a minority of the victims, most of whom died in the

provinces, often in conditions of civil war and sometimes with arms in their hands. In eighteen months or so the Frenchmen whom contemporaries regarded as monsters killed about as many of their countrymen as died in ten days of street-fighting and firing-squads in Paris in 1871. To take a different but equally revealing measure, the numbers of those who died in this year and a half are roughly twice those of the British soldiers who died on the first day of the battle of the Somme in 1916. Such bloodshed drove divisions even deeper between French groups, but their extent should not be exaggerated. All noblemen, perhaps, had lost something in the Revolution, but only a minority of them found it necessary to emigrate. Probably the clergy suffered more, man for man, than the nobility, and many priests fled abroad. Yet there were fewer emigrants from France during the Revolution than from the

American colonies after 1783. A much larger proportion of Americans felt too intimidated or disgusted with their Revolution to live in the United States after independence than the proportion of French people who could not live in France after the Terror.

CHANGES IN REVOLUTIONARY POLITICS

The Convention won victories and put down insurrection at home. By 1797, only Great Britain had not made peace with France, the Terror had been left behind, and the republic was ruled by something much more like a parliamentary régime under the constitution whose adoption closed the Convention era in 1796. The Revolution was safer than ever. But it did not seem so. Abroad, the royalists strove to get allies with whom to return and also intrigued with malcontents inside France. The return of the old order was a prospect which few in France would welcome, though. On the other hand, there were those who argued that the logic of democracy should be pressed further, that there were still great divisions between rich and poor which were as offensive as had been the old distinctions of legally privileged and unprivileged, and that the Parisian radicals should have a greater say in affairs. This was almost as alarming as fears of a restoration to those who had benefited from the Revolution or simply wanted to avoid further bloodshed. Thus pressed from Right and Left, the

Following the *coup d'état* of 9 November, 1799, the inauguration of a State Council, with Napoleon Bonaparte as First Consul, took place on 25 December. This event, which was to have such great significance for the whole of Europe, is portrayed here in one of the many later and non-contemporary pictures which glorified different episodes in what became the Napoleonic legend.

Directory (as the new régime was called) was in a way in a good position, though it made enemies who found the (somewhat zigzag) *via media* it followed unacceptable. In the end it was destroyed from within when a group of politicians intrigued with soldiers to bring about a *coup d'état* which instituted a new régime in 1799.

POST-REVOLUTIONARY FRANCE

IN 1799, TEN YEARS after the meeting of the Estates General, it was at least clear to most observers that France had for ever broken with the medieval past. In law this happened very rapidly. Nearly all the great

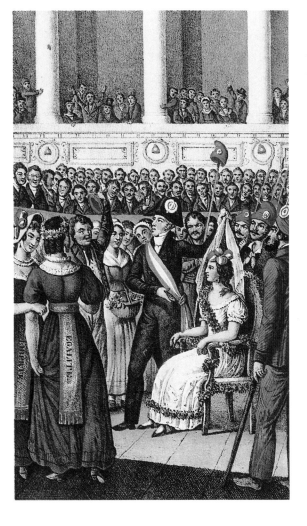

The prominent *sans-culotte* Pierre Chaumette (1763–1794) unveils the Altar to Reason in the cathedral of Notre Dame in November 1793.

reforms underlying it were legislated at least in principle in 1789. The formal abolition of feudalism, legal privilege and theocratic absolutism and the organization of society on individualist and secular foundations were the heart of the "principles of '89" then distilled in the Declaration of the Rights of Man and of the Citizen which prefaced the constitution of 1791. Legal equality and the legal protection of individual rights, the separation of Church and State and religious toleration were their expressions. The derivation of authority from popular sovereignty acting through a unified National Assembly, before whose legislation no privilege of locality or group could stand, was the basis of the jurisprudence which underlay them. It showed both that it could ride out financial storms far worse than those the old monarch had failed to master (national bankruptcy and the collapse of the currency among them), and that it could carry out administrative change of which enlightened despotism had only dreamed. Other Europeans watched aghast or at least amazed as this powerful legislative engine was employed to overturn and rebuild institutions at every level of French life. Legislative sovereignty was a great instrument of reform, as the enlightened despots had known. Judicial torture came to an end, and so did titular nobility, juridical inequality and the old corporate guilds of French workmen. Incipient trades unionism was scotched in the egg by legislation forbidding association by workers or employers for collective economic ends. In retrospect, the signposts to market society seem pretty plain. Even the old currency based on units in the Carolingian ratios of 1:20:12 (*livres*, *sous* and *deniers*) gave way to a decimal system of *francs* and *centimes*, just as the chaos of old-fashioned weights and measures was (in theory) replaced by the metric system later to become almost universal.

A church is desecrated during the French Revolution. In Paris, many important Christian icons were removed from churches or converted into revolutionary images by sculptors or painters. This included the changing of stone Bibles, held by statues of saints, into copies of the Declaration of the Rights of Man.

REVOLUTION AND THE CHURCH

Such great changes were bound to be divisive, the more so because people's minds change more slowly than their laws. Peasants who eagerly welcomed the abolition of feudal dues were much less happy about the disappearance of the communal usages from which they benefited and which were also part of the "feudal" order. Such conservatism was especially hard to interpret in religious affairs, yet was very important. The holy vessel kept at Rheims from which the kings of France had been anointed since the Middle Ages was publicly destroyed by the authorities during the Terror, an altar to Reason replaced the Christian one in the cathedral of Notre Dame and many priests underwent fierce personal persecution. Clearly, the France which did this was no longer Christian in the traditional sense, and the theocratic monarchy went unmourned by most of the French. Yet the treatment of the Church aroused popular opposition to the Revolution as nothing else had done, the cults of quasi-divinities such as Reason and the Supreme Being which some revolutionaries promoted were a flop, and many Frenchmen (and perhaps most Frenchwomen) would happily welcome the official restoration of the Catholic Church to French life when it eventually came. By then, it had long been restored de facto in the parishes by the spontaneous actions of French men and women.

A NEW DEBATE

The divisions aroused by revolutionary change in France could no more be confined within its borders than could the principles of '89. These had at first commanded much admiration and not much explicit condemnation or distrust in other countries, though this soon changed, in particular when French governments began to export their principles by propaganda and war. Change in France soon generated debate about what should happen in other countries. Such debate was bound to reflect the terminology and circumstances in which it arose. In this way France gave her politics to Europe and this is the second great fact about the revolutionary decade. That is when Modern European politics began, and the terms Right and Left have been with us ever since. Liberals and conservatives (though it was to be a decade or so before the terms were used) came into political existence when the French Revolution provided what appeared to be a touchstone or litmus paper for political standpoints. On one side were republicanism, a wide suffrage, individual rights, free speech and free publication; on the other were order, discipline, and emphasis on duties rather than rights, the recognition of the social function of hierarchy and a wish to temper market forces by morality.

The Tree of Liberty with the Devil Tempting John Bull was etched by British cartoonist James Gillray (1757–1815) to illustrate the failure of supposed attempts by English politicians to spread the revolution to Britain.

THE REVOLUTION'S EFFECTS BEYOND FRANCE

Some in France had always believed that the French Revolution had universal significance. In the language of enlightened thought they advocated the acceptance by other nations of the recipes they employed for the settlement of French problems. This was not entirely arrogant. Societies in pre-industrial and traditional Europe still had many features in common; all could learn something from France. In this way the forces making for French influence were reinforced by conscious propaganda and missionary effort. This was another route by which events in France entered universal history.

That the Revolution was of universal, unprecedented significance was not an idea confined to its admirers and supporters. It also lay at the roots of European conservatism as a self-conscious force. Well before 1789, it is true, many of the constituent elements of modern conservative thought were lying about in such phenomena as irritation over the reforming measures of enlightened despotism, clerical resentment of the prestige and effect of "advanced" ideas, and the emotional reaction from the fashionable and consciously rational which lay at the heart of romanticism. Such forces were especially prevalent in Germany, but it was in England that there appeared the first and in many ways the greatest statement of the conservative, anti-revolutionary argument. This was the *Reflections on the Revolution in France*, published in 1790 by Edmund Burke. As might easily be inferred from his former role as defender of the rights of the American colonists, this book was far from a mindless defence of privilege. In it a conservative stance shook itself clear of the legalistic defence of institutions and expressed itself in a theory of society as the creation of more

than will and reason and the embodiment of morality. The Revolution, by contrast, was condemned as the expression of the arrogance of the intellect, of arid rationalism, and of pride – deadliest of all the sins.

The new polarization which the Revolution brought to Europe's politics promoted also the new idea of revolution itself, and that was to have great consequences. The old idea that a political revolution was merely a circumstantial break in an essential continuity was replaced by one which took it as radical, comprehensive upheaval, leaving untouched no institution and limitless in principle, tending, perhaps, even to the subversion of such basic institutions as the family and property. According to whether people felt heartened or dismayed by this prospect, they sympathized with or deplored revolution wherever it occurred as a manifestation of a universal phenomenon. In the nineteenth century they came even to speak of *the* Revolution as a universally, eternally present

force. This idea was the extreme expression of an ideological form of politics which is by no means yet dead. There are still those who, broadly speaking, feel that all insurrectionary and subversive movements should, in principle, be approved or condemned without regard to the particular circumstances of cases. This mythology has produced much misery, but first Europe and then the world which Europe transformed have had to live with those who respond emotionally to it, just as earlier generations had to live with the follies of religious divisions. Its survival, unhappily, is testimony still of the impact of the French Revolution.

NAPOLEON BONAPARTE

MANY DATES CAN BE CHOSEN as the "beginning" of the French Revolution; a specific date to "end" it would be meaningless. The year 1799 none the less was an

This anonymous oil-painting shows the young Napoleon Bonaparte at Arcole (near Verona), where he defeated the Austrian army in November 1796.

important punctuation mark in its course. The *coup d'état* which then swept the Directory away brought to power a man who quickly inaugurated a dictatorship which was

to last until 1814 and turn international relations upside-down. This was Napoleon Bonaparte, formerly general of the republic, now First Consul of the new régime and soon to be the first Emperor of France. Like most of the leading figures of his age, he was still a young man when he came to power. He had already shown exceptional brilliance and ruthlessness as a soldier. His victories combined with a shrewd political sense and a readiness to act in an insubordinate manner to win him a glamorous reputation; in many ways he now seems the greatest example of the eighteenth-century type of "the adventurer". In 1799 he had a great personal prestige and popularity. No one except the defeated politicians much regretted it when he shouldered them aside and assumed power. Immediately he justified himself by defeating the Austrians (who had joined again in a war against France) and making a victorious peace for France (as he had done once already). This removed the threat to the Revolution; no one doubted Bonaparte's

Napoleon and his wife Joséphine are shown visiting the Sévane Brothers' factory in Rouen in November 1802.

The coronation of Napoleon Bonaparte (1769–1821) in Notre Dame is depicted by Jacques-Louis David.

own commitment to its principles. His consolidation of them was his most positive achievement.

NAPOLEONIC RULE

Although Napoleon (as he was called officially after 1804, when he proclaimed his empire) reinstituted monarchy in France, it was in no sense a restoration. Indeed, he took care so to affront the exiled Bourbon family that any reconciliation with it was inconceivable. He sought popular approval for the empire in a plebiscite and got it. This was a monarchy Frenchmen had voted for; it rested on popular sovereignty, that is, on the Revolution. It assumed the consolidation of the Revolution which the Consulate had already begun. All the great institutional reforms of the 1790s were confirmed or at least left intact; there was no disturbance of the land sales which had followed the confiscation of Church property, no resurrection of the old corporations, no questioning of the principle of equality before the law. Some measures were even taken further, notably when each department was given an administrative head, the prefect, who was in his powers something like one of the emergency emissaries of the Terror (many former revolutionaries became prefects). Such further centralization of the administrative structure would, of course, have been approved also by the enlightened despots. In the actual working of government, it is true, the principles of the Revolution were often infringed in practice. Like all his predecessors in power since 1793, Napoleon controlled the press by a punitive censorship, locked up people without trial and in general gave short shrift to the Rights of Man so far as civil liberties were concerned. Representative bodies existed under consulate and empire, but not much attention was paid to them. Yet it seems that this was what the French wanted, as they had wanted Napoleon's shrewd recognition of reality, a concordat with the pope which

Painted by Jacques-Louis David in 1801, this heroic portrait shows Napoleon crossing the Alps in April 1797, following in the path of Hannibal nearly 2,000 years before. Napoleon, always very aware of the importance of his public image, had instructed the great artist to portray him as a calm, strong figure astride a wild horse.

reconciled Catholics to the régime by giving legal recognition to what had already happened to the Church in France.

All in all, this amounted to a great consolidation of the Revolution and one guaranteed at home by firm government and by military and diplomatic strength abroad. Both were eventually to be eroded by Napoleon's huge military efforts. These for a time gave France the dominance of Europe; her armies fought their way to Moscow in the east and Portugal in the west and garrisoned the Atlantic and northern coast from Corunna to Stettin. Nevertheless, the cost of this was too great; even ruthless exploitation of occupied countries was not enough for France to sustain this hegemony indefinitely against the coalition of all the other European countries which Napoleon's arrogant assertion of his power aroused. When he invaded Russia in 1812 and the greatest army he ever led crumbled into ruins in the snows of the winter, he was doomed unless his enemies should fall out with one another. This time they did not. Napoleon himself blamed the British, who had been at war with him (and, before him, with the Revolution) with only one short break since 1792. There is something in this; the Anglo-French war was the last and most important round in a century of rivalry, as well as a war of constitutional monarchy against military dictatorship. It was the Royal Navy at Aboukir in 1798 and at Trafalgar in 1805 which confined Napoleon to Europe, British money which financed the allies when

they were ready to come forward, and a British army in the Iberian peninsula which kept alive there from 1809 onwards a front which drained French resources and gave hope to other Europeans.

NAPOLEON'S LEGACY

BY THE BEGINNING of 1814, Napoleon could defend only France. Although he did so at his most brilliant, the resources were not available to fight off Russian, Prussian and Austrian armies in the east, and a British invasion in the south-west. At last his generals and ministers were able to set him aside and make peace without a popular outcry, even though this meant the return of the Bourbons. But it could not by then mean the return of anything else of significance from the years before 1789. The Concordat remained, the departmental system remained, equality before the law remained, a represen-

The Prussian victory over the Napoleonic army at Katzbach on 26 August, 1813 is depicted in this painting.

tative system remained; the Revolution, in fact, had become part of the established order in France. Napoleon had provided the time, the social peace and the institutions for that to happen. Nothing survived of the Revolution except what he had confirmed.

This makes him very different from a monarch of the traditional stamp, even the most modernizing – and, in fact, he was often very conservative in his policies, distrusting innovation. In the end he was a democratic despot, whose authority came from the people, both in the formal sense of the plebiscites, and in the more general one that he had needed (and won) their goodwill to keep his armies in the field. He is thus nearer in style to twentieth-century rulers than to Louis XIV. Yet he shares with that monarch the credit for carrying French international power to an unprecedented height and because of this both of them have retained the admiration of their countrymen. But again there is an important, and twofold, difference: Napoleon not only dominated Europe as Louis XIV never did, but because the

Revolution had taken place his hegemony represented more than mere national supremacy, though this fact should not be sentimentalized. The Napoleon who was supposed to be a liberator and a great European was the creation of later legend. The most obvious impact he had on Europe between 1800 and 1814 was the bloodshed and upheaval he brought to every corner of it, often as a consequence of megalomania and personal vanity. But there were also important side-effects, some intentional, some not. They all added up to the further spread and effectiveness of the principles of the French Revolution.

THE REORGANIZATION OF GERMANY

The most obvious expression of the side-effects of Napoleon's rule was on the map. The patchwork quilt of the European state system of 1789 had undergone some revision already before Napoleon took power, when French armies in Italy, Switzerland and the United Provinces had created new satellite republics. But these had proved incapable of survival once French support was withdrawn and it was not until French hegemony was re-established under the Consulate that there appeared a new organization which would have enduring consequences in some parts of Europe. The most important of these were in west Germany whose political structure was revolutionized and medieval foundations swept away. German territories on the left bank of the Rhine were annexed to France for the whole of the period from 1801 to 1814, and this began a period of destroying historic German polities. Beyond the river, France provided the plan of a reorganization which secularized the ecclesiastical states, abolished nearly all the Free Cities, gave extra territory

Symbols of Napoleonic power are represented in this 19th-century illustration, which is now housed in the Biblioteca Nazionale in Turin, Italy.

Napoleonic Europe and the collapse of the French Empire

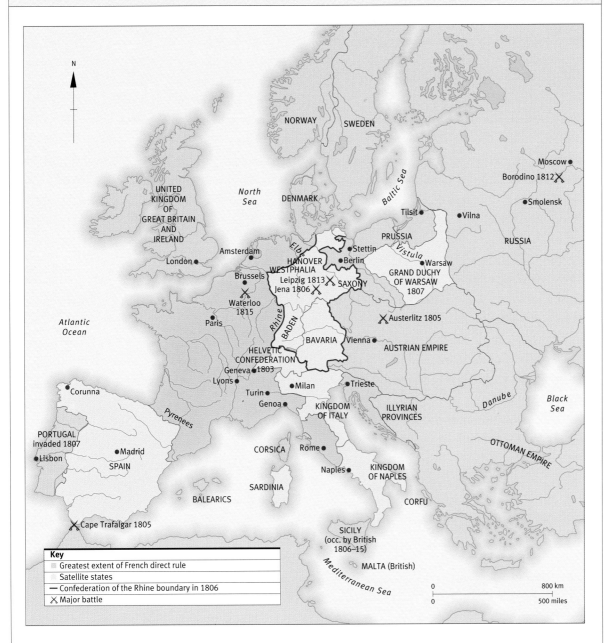

Key
- Greatest extent of French direct rule
- Satellite states
- — Confederation of the Rhine boundary in 1806
- ✕ Major battle

In 1812, the Napoleonic Empire had reached its greatest extent, but national feeling, both in the name of the *ancien régime* and in that of liberty and equality, was steadily building up against it. At home, the empire could win over neither the old French aristocracy nor the republicans, who could remember a time of greater freedom.

The Napoleonic bureaucracy was unable to control the smuggling and corruption that had emerged as a result of the continental blockade by Britain. Nor could it prevent prices from rising and the growing, dangerous opposition it faced from bankers. These divisive forces were underlined by the start of the Russian campaign which encouraged the formation of a new coalition (the sixth) between Russia, Britain and Prussia in 1813. At the beginning of the following year, the combined armies of Britain, Russia, Prussia, Austria and Sweden invaded France and by March they had occupied Paris. Napoleon abdicated and was exiled by the victors to the island of Elba.

to Prussia, Hanover, Bavaria and Baden to compensate them for losses elsewhere, and abolished the old independent imperial nobility. The practical effect was to diminish the Catholic and Habsburg influence in Germany while strengthening the influence of its larger princely states (especially Prussia). The constitution of the Holy Roman Empire was revised, too, to take account of these changes. In its new form it lasted only until 1806, when another defeat of the Austrians led to more changes in Germany and its abolition. So came to an end the institutional structure which, however inadequately, had given Germany such political coherence as it had possessed since Ottonian times. A Confederation of the Rhine was now set up which provided a third force balancing that of Prussia and Austria. Thus were triumphantly asserted the national interests of France in a great work of destruction. Richelieu and Louis XIV would have enjoyed the contemplation of a French frontier on the Rhine with, beyond it, a Germany divided into interests likely to hold one another in check. But there was another side to it; the old

structure, after all, had been a hindrance to German consolidation. No future rearrangement would ever contemplate the resurrection of the old structures. When, finally, the allies came to settle post-Napoleonic Europe, they too provided for a German Confederation. It was different from Napoleon's. Prussia and Austria were members of it in so far as their territories were German, but there was no going back on the fact of consolidation. A complicated structure of over three hundred political units with different principles of organization in 1789 was reduced to thirty-eight states in 1815.

THE REORGANIZATION OF ITALY AND OTHER STATES

Reorganization was less dramatic in Italy and its effects less revolutionary. The Napoleonic system provided in the north and south of the peninsula two large units which were nominally independent, while a large part of it (including the Papal States) was formally incorporated in France and organized in departments. None of this structure survived in 1815, but neither was there a complete restoration of the old régime. In particular, the ancient republics of Genoa and Venice were left in the tombs to which the armies of the Directory had first consigned them. They were absorbed by bigger states, Genoa by Sardinia, Venice by Austria. Elsewhere in Europe, at the height of Napoleonic power, France had annexed and governed directly a huge block of territory whose coasts ran from the Pyrenees to Denmark in the north and from Catalonia almost without interruption to the boundary between Rome and Naples in the south. Lying detached from it was a large piece of modern Yugoslavia. Satellite states and vassals of varying degrees of real independence, some of them ruled over by

In this 19th-century painting an Austrian soldier bids his family farewell as he leaves to fight the Napoleonic army during the Austrian rebellion against French rule of 1813–1815.

Nationalist feelings ran high in European countries under French occupation. One of the most famous pictures by the great Spanish artist Francisco de Goya (1746–1828) had as its subject the popular Madrid rising of 1808 against the French garrison.

members of Napoleon's own family, divided between them the rest of Italy, Switzerland and Germany west of the Elbe. Isolated in the east was another satellite, the "grand duchy" of Warsaw, which had been created from former Russian territory.

THE FRENCH EMPIRE

In most of these countries common administrative practice and institutions provided a large measure of shared experience. That experience, of course, was of institutions and ideas which embodied the principles of the Revolution. They hardly reached beyond the Elbe except in the brief Polish experiment and thus the French Revolution came to be another of those great shaping influences which again and again have helped to differentiate Eastern and Western Europe. Within the French Empire, Germans, Italians, Illyrians, Belgians and Dutch were all governed by the Napoleonic legal codes; the bringing of these to fruition was the result of Napoleon's own initiative and insistence, but the work was essentially that of revolutionary legislators who had never been able in the troubled 1790s to draw up the new codes so many in France had hoped for in 1789. With the codes went concepts of family, property, the individual, public power and others which were thus generally spread through Europe. They sometimes replaced and sometimes supplemented a chaos of local, customary, Roman and ecclesiastical law. Similarly, the departmental system of the empire imposed a common administrative practice, service in the French armies imposed a common discipline and military regulation,

A contemporary illustration depicts Napoleon landing on the French coast in February 1815, after his flight from exile in Elba.

and French weights and measures, based on the decimal system, replaced many local scales. Such innovations exercised an influence beyond the actual limits of French rule, providing models and inspiration to modernizers in other countries. The models were all the more easily assimilated because French officials and technicians worked in many of the satellites while many nationalities other than French were represented in the Napoleonic service.

THE DISPERSION OF REVOLUTIONARY IDEALS

Changes took time to produce their full effect in the French Empire, but it was a deep one and was revolutionary. It was by no means necessarily liberal; even if the Rights of Man formally followed the Tricolour of the French armies, so did Napoleon's secret police, quartermasters and customs officers. A more

subtle revolution, deriving from the Napoleonic impact, lay in the reaction and resistance it provoked. In spreading revolutionary principles the French were often putting a rod in pickle for their own backs. Popular sovereignty lay at the heart of the Revolution and it is an ideal closely linked to that of nationalism. French principles said that peoples ought to govern themselves and that the proper unit in which they should do so was the nation: the revolutionaries had proclaimed their own republic "one and indivisible" for this reason. Many of their foreign admirers applied this principle to their own countries; manifestly, Italians and Germans did not live in national states, and perhaps they should. But this was only one side of the coin. French Europe was run for the benefit of France, and it thus denied the national rights of other Europeans. They saw their agriculture and commerce sacrificed to French economic policy, found they had to serve in the French armies, or to receive at the hands of Napoleon French (or Quisling) rulers and viceroys. When even those who had welcomed the principles of the Revolution felt such things as grievances, it is hardly surprising that those who had never welcomed them at all should begin to think in terms of national resistance, too. Nationalism in Europe was given an immense fillip by the Napoleonic era, even if governments distrusted it and felt uneasy about employing it. Germans began to think of themselves as more than Westphalians and Bavarians, and Italians began to believe they were more than Romans or Milanese, because they discerned a common interest against France. In Spain and Russia the identification of patriotic resistance with resistance to the Revolution was virtually complete.

THE BATTLE OF WATERLOO

In the end, then, though the dynasty Napoleon hoped to found and the empire he set up both proved fragile, his work was of great importance. He unlocked huge reserves of energy in other countries just as the Revolution had unlocked them in France, and afterwards they could never be quite shut up again. He ensured the legacy of the Revolution its maximum effect and this was his greatest achievement, whether he desired it or not.

His unconditional abdication in 1814 was not quite the end of the story. Just under a year later the emperor returned to France from Elba where he had lived in a pensioned exile, and the restored Bourbon régime crumbled at a touch. The allies none the less determined to overthrow him, for he had frightened them too much in the past. Napoleon's attempt to anticipate the gathering of overwhelming forces against him came to an end at Waterloo, on 18 June, 1815, when the threat of a revived French Empire was destroyed by the Anglo-Belgian and Prussian armies. This time the victors sent him to St Helena, thousands of miles away in the South Atlantic, where he died in 1821.

The Battle of Waterloo – a scene from which is depicted in this contemporary illustration – finally broke the power of Napoleon's army. The French suffered 25,000 casualties, and the allies nearly as many.

The final alarm that he had given them strengthened their determination to make a peace that would avoid any danger of a repetition of the quarter-century of almost continuous war which Europe had undergone in the wake of the Revolution. Thus Napoleon still shaped the map of Europe, not only by the changes he had made in it, but also by the fear France had inspired under his leadership.

This detail from a 19th-century French painting depicts an imaginary scene of Napoleon being greeted by his soldiers on his return from Elba in February 1815.

4 POLITICAL CHANGE: A NEW EUROPE

WHATEVER CONSERVATIVE statesmen hoped in 1815, an uncomfortable and turbulent era had only just begun. This can be seen most easily in the way the map of Europe changed in the next sixty years. By 1871, when a newly united Germany took its place among the great powers, most of Europe west of a line drawn from the Adriatic to the Baltic was organized in states based on the principle of nationality, even if some minorities still denied it. Even to the east of that line there were some states which were already identified with nations. By 1914 the triumph of nationalism was to go further still, and most of the Balkans would be organized as nation-states, too.

NATIONALISM

Nationalism, one aspect of a new kind of politics, had origins which went back a long way, to the examples set in Great Britain and some of Europe's smaller states in earlier times. Yet its great triumphs were to come after 1815, as part of the appearance of a new politics. At their heart lay an acceptance of a new framework of thought which recognized the existence of a public interest greater than that of individual rulers or privileged hierarchies. It also assumed that competition to define and protect that interest was legitimate. Such competition was thought increasingly to require special arenas and

A contemporary illustration depicts the 1815 Congress of Vienna, which followed the defeat of the Napoleonic Empire. Every important decision at the congress was taken by the victors, although France was allowed to attend. Prussia was allotted new provinces in the Rhineland, the mineral resources of which later helped Prussia to become the strongest German power.

institutions; old juridical or courtly forms no longer seemed sufficient to settle political questions.

An institutional framework for this transformation of public life took longer to emerge in some countries than others. Even in the most advanced it cannot be identified with any single set of practices. It always tended, though, to be strongly linked with the recognition and promotion of certain principles. Nationalism was one of them which told most against older principles – that of dynasticism, for instance. It was more and more a commonplace of European political discourse, as the nineteenth century went on, that the interests of those recognized to be "historic" nations should be protected and promoted by governments. This was, of course, wholly compatible with bitter and prolonged disagreement about which nations were historic, how their interests should be defined, and to what extent they could and should be given weight in statesmen's decisions.

THE GROWING POWER OF THE STATE

There were also other principles in play besides nationalism. Terms like democracy and liberalism do not help very much in defining them, though they must be used in default of better ones. In most countries there was a general trend towards accepting representative institutions as a way of associating (even if only formally) more and more people with the government. Liberals and democrats almost always asked for more people to be given votes and for better electoral representation. More and more, too, the individual became the basis of political and social organization in economically advanced countries. The individual's membership of communal,

Political liberty in post-Napoleonic Europe was championed by the English poet Lord Byron, shown here in a portrait that captures his romantic aura. He died of malaria at the age of 36, attempting to aid the Greek struggle to throw off Turkish rule.

Time chart (1789–1870)

	1789 The French Revolution		1848 Revolutions across Europe	1853–1856 The Crimean War	1861 Abolition of serfdom in Russia War of Secession in America	1870 Franco-Prussian War Third Republic in France
1800						**1900**
	1815 Waterloo Vienna Congress: Restoration	1830 July Revolution in Paris	1852 Second Empire in France	1859 Beginning of the unification of Italy	1863 Polish uprising	1866 Austro-Prussian War

religious, occupational and family units came to matter much less than his or her individual rights. Though this led in some ways to greater freedom, it sometimes led to less. The state became much more juridically powerful in relation to its subjects in the nineteenth century than ever before, and slowly, as its apparatus became technically more efficient, came to be able to coerce them more effectively.

THE IMPACT OF THE FRENCH REVOLUTION

The French Revolution had been of enormous importance in actually launching such changes but its continuing influence as example and a source of mythology mattered just as much. For all the hopes and fears that the Revolution was over by 1815, its full Europe-wide impact was then still to come. In many other countries institutions already swept away in France invited criticism and demolition. They were the more vulnerable because other forces of economic and social change were also at work. This gave revolutionary ideas and traditions new opportunities. There was a widespread sense that all Europe faced, for good or ill, potential revolution. This encouraged the upholders and would-be destroyers of the existing order alike to sharpen political issues and fit them into the frameworks of the

Europe in 1815

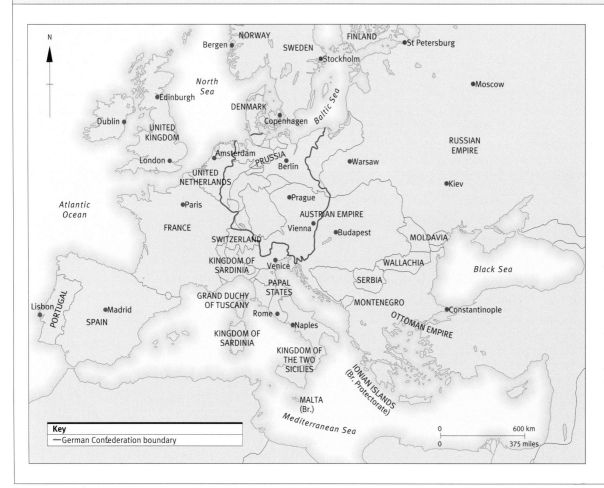

In Vienna, Europe was shared out, and France lost a large portion of the territory she had occupied between 1792 and 1814. Prussia, Austria and Russia increased their territories; Belgium and the Netherlands became the United Netherlands, and Norway and Sweden were united. The Grand Duchy of Warsaw disappeared. A new Germanic Confederation of 38 sovereign states and three kingdoms appeared, and Britain retained Malta and the Ionian Islands.

principles of 1789, nationalism and liberalism. By and large, these ideas dominated the history of Europe down to about 1870 and provided the dynamic of its politics. They did not achieve all their advocates hoped. Their realization in practice had many qualifications, they frequently and thwartingly got in one another's way, and they had many opponents. Yet they remain useful guiding threads in the rich and turbulent history of nineteenth-century Europe, already a political laboratory whose experiments, explosions and discoveries were changing the history of the rest of the world.

THE TREATY OF VIENNA

The influences of nationalism and liberalism could already be seen at work in the negotiations shaping the foundation deed of the nineteenth-century international order, the Treaty of Vienna of 1815, which closed the era of the French wars. Its central aim was to prevent their repetition. The peacemakers sought the containment of France and the avoidance of revolution, using as their materials the principle of legitimacy which was the ideological core of conservative Europe and certain practical territorial arrangements against future French aggression. Thus Prussia was given large acquisitions on the Rhine, a new northern state appeared under a Dutch king ruling both Belgium and the Netherlands, the kingdom of Sardinia was given Genoa, and Austria not only recovered her former Italian possessions, but kept Venice and was allowed a virtually free hand in keeping the other Italian states in order. In most of these cases legitimacy bowed to expediency; those despoiled by the revolutionaries or Napoleon did not obtain restoration. But the powers talked legitimacy all the same, and (once the arrangements were complete) did so

with some success. For nearly forty years the Vienna settlement provided a framework within which disputes were settled without war. Most of the régimes installed in 1815 were still there, even if some of them were somewhat shaken, forty years later.

This owed much to the salutary fear of revolution. In all the major continental states the restoration era (as the years after 1815 have been termed) was a great period for policemen and plotters alike. Secret societies proliferated, undiscouraged by failure after failure. This record showed, though, that there was no subversive threat that could not be handled easily enough. Austrian troops dealt with attempted coups in Piedmont and Naples, French soldiers restored the power of a reactionary Spanish king hampered by a liberal constitution, the Russian empire survived a military conspiracy and a Polish revolt. The Austrian predominance in Germany was not threatened at all and it is difficult in retrospect to discern any very real danger to any part of the Habsburg monarchy before 1848. Russian and Austrian power, the first in reserve, the second the main force in Central Europe and Italy from 1815 to 1848, were the two rocks on which the Vienna system rested.

A satirical French cartoon depicts the key protagonists of the Congress of Vienna. The British foreign secretary Robert Castlereagh (second left) fought for the creation of the Quadruple Alliance of Britain, Austria, Prussia and Russia. Representatives of these four countries were to meet regularly in order to guarantee "the maintenance of the peace of Europe".

Mistakenly, liberalism and nationalism were usually supposed to be inseparable; this was to prove terribly untrue in later times, but in so far as a few people did seek to change Europe by revolution before 1848, it is broadly true that they wanted to do so by advancing both the political principles of the French Revolution – representative government, popular sovereignty, freedom of the individual and the press – and those of nationality. Many confused the two; the most famous and admired of those who did so was Mazzini, a young Italian. By advocating an Italian unity most of his countrymen did not want and conspiring unsuccessfully to bring it about, he became an inspiration and model for other nationalists and democrats in every continent for over a century and one of the first idols of radical chic. The age of the ideas he represented had not yet come.

RESTORATION IN FRANCE

To the west of the Rhine, where the writ of the Holy Alliance (as was termed the group of three conservative powers, Russia, Austria and Prussia) did not run, the story was different; there, legitimism was not to last long. The very restoration of the Bourbon dynasty in 1814 had itself been a compromise with the principle of legitimacy. Louis XVIII was supposed to have reigned like any other king of France since the death of his predecessor, Louis XVII, in a Paris prison in 1795. In fact, as everyone knew but legitimists tried to conceal, he came back in the baggage train of the Allied armies which had defeated Napoleon and he only did so on terms acceptable to the French political and military élites of the Napoleonic period and, presumably, tolerable by the majority of the French. The

This heroic portrayal of the July Revolution of 1830 in France, *Liberty Leading the People*, was painted by Eugène Delacroix (1798–1863).

An English painting depicts Louis XVIII's return to France in 1814 after 23 years in exile. His 10-year reign was characterized by moderation and respect for the revolutionary institutions and the Napoleonic Code.

restored régime was regulated by a charter which created a constitutional monarchy, albeit with a limited suffrage. The rights of individuals were guaranteed and the land settlement resulting from revolutionary confiscations and sales was unquestioned; there was to be no return to 1789.

Nevertheless, there was some uncertainty about the future; battle between Right and Left began with arguments about the charter itself – was it a contract between king and people, or a simple emanation of the royal benevolence which might therefore be withdrawn as easily as it had been granted? – and went on over a whole range of issues which raised questions of principle (or were thought to do so) about ground won for liberty and the possessing classes in the Revolution.

CHARLES X IS DEPOSED

What was implicitly at stake was what the Revolution had actually achieved. One way of describing that would be to say that those who had struggled to be recognized as having a voice in ruling France under the *ancien régime* had won; the political weight of the "notables", as they were sometimes called, was assured and they, whether drawn from the old nobility of France, those who had done well out of the Revolution, Napoleon's lackeys, or simply substantial landowners and businessmen, were now the real rulers of France. Another change had been the nation-making brought about in French institutions; no person or corporation could now claim to stand outside the operative sphere of the national government of France. Finally and crucially, the Revolution had changed French political thinking. Among other things, the terms in which French public affairs would be discussed and debated had been transformed. Wherever the line was to be drawn between Right and Left, conservatives or liberals, it was on that line that political battle now had to be centred, not over the privilege of counselling a monarch by Divine Right. This was just what the last king of the direct Bourbon line, Charles X, failed to see. He foolishly attempted to break out of the constitutional limitations which bound him, by what was virtually a *coup d'état*. Paris rose against him in the "July Revolution" of 1830, liberal politicians hastily put themselves at its head, and to the chagrin of republicans, ensured that a new king replaced Charles.

LOUIS PHILIPPE

Louis Philippe was head of the junior branch of the French royal house, the Orléans family, but to many conservative eyes he was the Revolution incarnate. His father had voted for the execution of Louis XVI (and went to the scaffold himself soon after) while the new king had fought as an officer in the republican armies. He had even been a member of the notorious Jacobin club which was widely believed to have been a deep-rooted conspiracy, and certainly had been a forcing-house for some of the Revolution's most prominent leaders. To liberals Louis Philippe was attractive for much the same reasons; he reconciled the Revolution with the stability provided by

This scene is from the "glorious days" of the French "July Revolution" of 1830. There was substantial popular feeling against Charles X in Paris at a time when widespread recession and unemployment meant that more than 25 per cent of the city's inhabitants were claiming public assistance.

Restoration

"Once Napoleon was dead, divine and human powers recovered, but there was no faith in them. ...

"Until then, there had been people who hated nobles, cried out against the clergy, who conspired against kings; there had been shouts against abuse and prejudice, but it was a great novelty to see the people smile. If a noble, a clergyman or a king went by, the peasants who had fought in the war began to shake their heads and say, 'Oh we've seen him at another place and time, but he had a different face!', and when the throne and the altar were mentioned, they answered, 'Those are only a few lengths of wood, we have nailed them together and unnailed them', and when they were told, 'People, you have mended your ways, you have called back your kings and your clergy', they answered, 'We didn't, not those charlatans', and when it was suggested, 'People, forget the past, work and obey', they shifted in their seats and there was a dull sound of resentment. It was no more than a rusty, nicked sword shaking in the corner of the hut, but then, one hurried to add, 'At least stay where you are; if no-one troubles you, don't look for trouble.' Unfortunately, they were content with that.

"All the sicknesses of the current century come from two sources: the people who have gone through '93 and 1814 have two wounds in their hearts. All that was, is no longer; and that will be, is not yet. Do not look any further for the secret of our troubles."

An extract from *Confessions of a Child of the Century* (1835) by Alfred de Musset (1810–1857).

monarchy, though the left wing were disappointed. The régime over which he was to preside for eighteen years proved unimpeachably constitutional and preserved essential political freedoms, but protected the interests of the well-to-do. It vigorously suppressed urban disorder (of which poverty produced

Louis Philippe d'Orléans (1773–1850) and his five sons are depicted leaving Versailles after a military parade in this picture by the French painter Horace Vernet (1789–1863).

plenty in the 1830s) and this made it unpopular with the Left. One prominent politician told his fellow-countrymen to enrich themselves – a recommendation much ridiculed and misunderstood, though all he was trying to do was to tell them that the way to obtain the vote was through the qualification which a high income conferred (in 1830 only about a third as many Frenchmen as Englishmen had a vote for their national representatives, while the population of France was about twice that of England). Nevertheless, in theory, the July Monarchy rested on popular sovereignty, the revolutionary principle of 1789.

EUROPE IN THE 1830s

The July Monarchy's revolutionary base gave it a certain special international standing in a Europe divided by ideology. In the 1830s there were sharply evident differences between a Europe of constitutional states – Britain, France, Spain and Portugal – and that of the legitimist, dynastic states of the East, with their Italian and German satellites. Conservative governments had not liked the July revolution. They were alarmed when the Belgians rebelled against their Dutch king in 1830, but could not support him because the British and French favoured the Belgians and

The fall of Missolonghi to the Turks in 1826 is represented by this personification of Greece on the ruins of the city, by Eugène Delacroix. In 1827 Britain, France and Russia sent a navy against the Turkish fleet in an effort to help the Greeks gain their independence.

Russia had a Polish rebellion on her hands. It took until 1839 to secure the establishment of an independent Belgium, and this was until 1848 the only important change in the state system created by the Vienna settlement, though the internal troubles of Spain and Portugal caused ripples which troubled European diplomacy.

THE EASTERN QUESTION

Elsewhere, in south-east Europe, the pace of change was quickening. A new revolutionary era was opening there just as that of Western Europe moved to its climax. In 1804 a well-to-do Serbian pork dealer had led a revolt by his countrymen against the undisciplined Turkish garrison of Belgrade. At that

One of the first Turkish reactions to the Greek declaration of independence was the Massacre of Chios in 1822. Eugène Delacroix produced moving paintings of the massacre – such as this one – which epitomized the Romantic school of painting.

moment, the Ottoman régime was willing to countenance his actions in order to bridle its own mutinous soldiers. But the eventual cost to the empire was the establishment of an autonomous Serbian princedom in 1817. By then the Turks had also ceded Bessarabia to Russia, and had been forced to recognize that their hold on much of Greece and Albania was little more than formal, real power being in the hands of the local pashas.

This was, though hardly yet visibly so, the opening of the Eastern Question of the nineteenth century: who or what was to inherit the fragments of the crumbling Ottoman Empire? It was to take more than a century and a world war to solve the question in Europe; in what were once Asian provinces of the empire, the wars of the Ottoman Succession are still going on today. Racial, religious, ideological, and diplomatic issues were entangled from the start. The Vienna settlement did not include Ottoman territories among those covered by guarantees from the great powers. When what was soon represented as a "revolution" of "Greeks" (that is, Orthodox Christian subjects of the sultan, many of whom were bandits and pirates) began against the Turks in 1821, Russia favoured the rebels; this cut across conservative principles, but religion and the old pull of Russian imperialist expansion to the southeast made it impossible for the Holy Alliance to support the sultan as it supported other rulers. In the end, the Russians went to war with the Ottomans and defeated them. It was now evident that the nineteenth-century Eastern Question was going to be further complicated by nationalism, for the new kingdom of Greece which emerged in 1832 was bound to give ideas to other peoples in the Balkans.

THE REVOLUTIONS OF 1848

IN 1848 CAME a new revolutionary explosion. Briefly, it seemed that the whole 1815 settlement was in jeopardy. The 1840s had been years of economic hardship, food shortages and distress in many places, particularly in Ireland where, in 1846, there was a great famine, and then in Central Europe and France in 1847, where a commercial slump starved the cities. Unemployment was widespread. This bred violence which gave new edge to radical movements everywhere. One disturbance inspired another; example was contagious and weakened the capacity of the international security system to deal with further outbreaks. The symbolic start came in February, in Paris, where Louis Philippe abdicated after discovering the middle classes would no longer support his continued

Czechs, Croats, Slovaks, Poles, Hungarians, Italians and Austrians rebelled in 1848, demanding independence from the Austrian government and recognition of their national identities. This 1848 painting shows the national guard trying to restore order to the streets of Vienna.

A united Italy is proclaimed in 1849. Led by Giuseppe Mazzini, the Roman Republic, as it was known, forced Pope Pius IX to flee, but the uprising was defeated by French troops in 1850. Mazzini's influence declined, although he became an inspiration to later Italian patriots.

opposition to the extension of the suffrage. By the middle of the year, government had been swept aside or was at best on the defensive in every major European capital except London and St Petersburg. When a republic appeared in France after the February Revolution every revolutionary and political exile in Europe had taken heart. The dreams of thirty years' conspiracies seemed realizable. The *Grande Nation* would be on the move again and the armies of the Great Revolution might march once more to spread its principles. What happened, though, was very different. France made a diplomatic genuflexion in the direction of martyred Poland, the classical focus of liberal sympathies, but the only military operations it undertook were in defence of the pope, an unimpeachably conservative cause.

This was symptomatic. The revolutionaries of 1848 were provoked by very different situations, and many different aims, and followed divergent and confusing paths. In most of Italy and Central Europe they rebelled against governments which they thought oppressive because they were illiberal; there, the great symbolic demand was for constitu-

tions to guarantee essential freedoms. When such a revolution occurred in Vienna itself, the chancellor Metternich, architect of the conservative order of 1815, fled into exile. Successful revolution at Vienna meant the paralysis and therefore the dislocation of the whole of Central Europe. Germans were now free to have their revolutions without fear of Austrian intervention in support of the *ancien régime* in the smaller states. So were other peoples within the Austrian dominions; Italians (led by an ambitious but apprehensive conservative king of Sardinia) turned on the Austrian armies in Lombardy and Venetia, Hungarians revolted at Budapest, and Czechs at Prague. This much complicated things. Many of these revolutionaries wanted national independence rather than constitutionalism, though constitutionalism seemed for a time the way to independence because it attacked dynastic autocracy.

THE FAILURES OF 1848

If the liberals were successful in getting constitutional governments installed in all the capitals of Central Europe and Italy, then it followed there would actually come into existence nations hitherto without state structures of their own, or at least without them for a very long time. If Slavs achieved their own national liberation then states previously thought of as German would be shorn of huge tracts of their territory, notably in Poland and Bohemia. It took some time for this to sink in. The German liberals suddenly fell over this problem in 1848 and quickly drew their conclusions; they chose nationalism. (The Italians were still to be coming to terms with their own version of the dilemma in the South Tyrol a hundred years later.) The German revolutions of 1848 failed, essentially, because the German liberals decided that German nationalism required the preservation of German lands in the east. Hence, they needed a strong Prussia and must accept its terms for the future of Germany. There were other signs, too, that the tide had turned before the end of 1848. The Austrian army had mastered the Italians. In Paris a rising aiming to give the Revolution a further shove in the direction of democracy was crushed with great bloodshed in June. The republic was, after all, to be a conservative one. In 1849 came the end. The Austrians overthrew the Sardinian army which was the only shield of the Italian revolutions, and monarchs all over the peninsula then began to withdraw the constitutional concessions they had made while Austrian power was in abeyance. German rulers did the same, led by Prussia. The pressure was kept up on the Habsburgs by the Croats and Hungarians, but then the Russian army came to its ally's help.

THE SPRINGTIME OF THE NATIONS

Liberals saw 1848 as a "springtime of the nations". If it was one, the shoots had not lived long before they withered. By the end of 1849 the formal structure of Europe was once again much as it had been in 1847, in spite of important changes within some countries. Nationalism had certainly been a popular cause in 1848, but it had been shown that it was neither strong enough to sustain revolutionary governments nor necessarily an enlightened force. Its failure shows the charge that the statesmen of 1815 "neglected" to give it due attention is false; no new nation emerged from 1848 for none was ready to do so. The basic reason for this was that although nationalities might exist, over most of Europe nationalism was still an abstraction for the masses; only relatively few and well-

The Italian nationalist leader Giuseppe Mazzini (1805–1872), pictured here, continued to campaign for an Italian republic after the country was unified as a monarchy.

Six hundred delegates attended the meeting of the German National Assembly in Frankfurt in 1848. The assembly had a significantly nationalistic character – some of its members proposed the formation of a Greater Germany, which would include the Tyrol, Bohemia, Alsace, Switzerland and the Netherlands.

High levels of unemployment and rapid inflation caused starvation in Poland during 1845–1847, which led to rioting in the cities. This contemporary painting shows angry crowds storming the public bakery in Breslau Market.

educated, or at least half-educated, people much cared about it. Where national differences also embodied social issues there was sometimes effective action by people who felt they had an identity given them by language, tradition or religion, but it did not lead to the setting up of new nations. The Ruthene peasants of Galicia in 1847 had happily murdered their Polish landlords when the Habsburg administration allowed them to do so. Having thus satisfied themselves they remained loyal to the Habsburgs in 1848.

POPULAR UPRISINGS

There were some genuinely popular risings in 1848. In Italy they were usually revolts of townsmen rather than peasants; the Lombard peasants, indeed, cheered the Austrian army when it returned, because they saw no good for them in a revolution led by the aristocrats who were their landlords. In parts of Germany, over much of which the traditional structures of landed rural society remained intact, the peasants behaved as their predecessors had done in France in 1789, burning their landlords' houses, not merely through personal animus but in order to destroy the hated and feared records of rents, dues and labour services. Such outbreaks frightened urban liberals as much as the Parisian outbreak of despair and unemployment in the June Days frightened the middle classes in France. There, because the peasant was since 1789 (speaking broadly) a conservative, the government was assured the support of the provinces in crushing the Parisian poor who had given radicalism its brief success. But conservatism could be found within revolutionary movements, too.

German working-class turbulence alarmed the better-off, but this was because the leaders of German workers talked of "socialism" while actually seeking a return to the past. They had the safe world of guilds and apprenticeships in mind, and feared machinery in factories, steamboats on the Rhine which put boatmen out of work, the opening of unrestricted entry to trades – in short, the all-too-evident signs of the onset of market society. Almost always, liberalism's lack of appeal to the masses was shown up in 1848 by popular revolution.

THE REPERCUSSIONS OF 1848

Altogether, the social importance of 1848 is as complex and escapes easy generalization as much as its political content. It was probably in the countryside of Eastern and Central Europe that the revolutions changed society most. There, liberal principles and the fear of popular revolt went hand in hand to impose change on the landlords. Wherever outside Russia obligatory peasant labour and bondage to the soil survived, it was abolished as a result of 1848. That year carried the rural social revolution launched sixty years earlier in France to its conclusion in Central and most of Eastern Europe. The way was now open for the reconstruction of agricultural life in Germany and the Danube valley on individualist and market lines. Though many of its practices and habits of mind were still to linger, feudal society had in effect now come to an end all over Europe. The political components of French revolutionary principles, though, would have to wait longer for their expression.

The Venetian Republic is proclaimed in St Mark's Square on 23 March, 1848, freeing Venice from Austrian rule.

THE CRIMEAN WAR

In the case of nationalism this was not very long. A dispute over Russian influence in the Near East, where Turkish power was visibly declining, in 1854 ended the long peace between great powers which had lasted since 1815. The Crimean War, in which the French and British fought as allies of the Turks against the Russians, was in many ways a notable struggle. Fighting took place in the Baltic, in southern Russia, and in the Crimea, the last theatre attracting most attention. There, the allies had set themselves to capture Sebastopol, the naval base which was the key to Russian power in the Black Sea. Some of

the results were surprising. The British army fought gallantly, as did its opponents and allies, but was especially distinguished by the inadequacy of its administrative arrangements; the scandal these caused launched an important wave of radical reform at home. Incidentally the war also helped to found the prestige of a new profession for women, that of nursing, for the collapse of British medical services had been particularly striking. Florence Nightingale's work launched the first major extension of the occupational opportunities available to respectable women since the creation of female religious communities in the Dark Ages. The conduct of the war is also noteworthy in another way as an

A montage illustrates the defence of Sebastopol, the Crimean port that was captured from the Russians in September 1855 after a long struggle. The Crimean War was notable for its enormous number of casualties – more than resulted from any other European war between 1815 and 1914. Of the 675,000 fatalities of the Crimean War, more than 80 per cent were caused by disease or infected wounds.

The consequences of the Crimean War

The Crimean War broke out in 1853. The conflict escalated in the following year and lasted until 1856. Russian interest in the Turkish Straits, which would allow them an outlet to the Mediterranean, brought them into direct conflict with the British, who claimed that the Straits must be kept open to international traffic (a position that was vital for a country like Britain, which drew its strength from maritime control and from its powerful navy).

By 1855, the Russian troops were clearly fighting a losing battle against the Turkish, British and French allied forces. When Tsar Nicholas I died that year, his successor, Alexander II, recognized that he had no choice but to sue for peace.

The signatories of the peace treaty of Paris in 1856 agreed to maintain "the integrity of the Turkish Empire". Russia ceded the left bank of the mouth of the Danube to Moldavia. Moldavia and Wallachia (which was united with Romania in 1858) and Serbia were recognized as self-governing principalities under the protection of the European powers. Russia ceased to have the right to maintain warships in the Black Sea and the Danube was to be open to commercial navigation from every nation.

A British position to the east of Sebastopol is depicted in this Crimean War engraving.

index of modernity: it was the first between major powers in which steamships and a railway were employed.

Yet these things, however portentous, mattered less in the short run than what the war did to international relations. Russia was defeated and her long enjoyment of a power to intimidate Turkey was bridled for a time. A step was taken towards the establishment of another new Christian nation, Romania, which was finally brought about in 1862. Once more, nationality triumphed in former Turkish lands. But the crucial effect of the war was that the Holy Alliance had disappeared. The old rivalry of the eighteenth century between Austria and Russia over what would happen to the Turkish inheritance in the Balkans had broken out again when Austria warned Russia not to occupy the Danube principalities (as the future Romania was termed) during the war and then occupied them herself. This was five years after Russia had intervened to restore Habsburg power by crushing the Hungarian revolution. It was the end of friendship between the two powers. The next time Austria faced a threat she would have to do so without the Russian policeman of conservative Europe at her side.

Napoleon III (1808–1873), formerly Louis-Napoleon Bonaparte, was president of the French Republic and in 1852 proclaimed himself ruler of the Second Empire.

NAPOLEON III

In 1856, when peace was made, few people can have anticipated how quickly the next threat to Austria would come. Within ten years Austria lost in two short, sharp wars her hegemony both in Italy and in Germany, and those countries were united in new national states. Nationalism had indeed triumphed, and at the cost of the Habsburgs, as had been prophesied by enthusiasts in 1848, but in a totally unexpected way. Not revolution, but the ambitions of two traditionally expansive monarchical states, Sardinia and Prussia, had led each to set about improving its position at the expense of Austria, whose isolation was at that moment complete. Not only had she sacrificed the Russian alliance, but after 1852 France was ruled by an emperor who again bore the name Napoleon (he was the nephew of the first to do so). He had been elected president of the Second Republic, whose constitution he then set aside by *coup d'état*. The name Napoleon was itself terrifying. It suggested a programme of international reconstruction – or revolution. Napoleon III (the second was a legal fiction, a son of Napoleon I who had never ruled) stood for the destruction of the anti-French settlement of 1815 and therefore of the Austrian predominance which propped it up in Italy and Germany. He talked the language of nationalism with less inhibition than most rulers and seems to have believed in it. With arms and diplomacy he forwarded the work of two great diplomatic technicians, Cavour and Bismarck, the prime ministers respectively of Sardinia and of Prussia.

UNITY IN ITALY AND GERMANY

In 1859 Sardinia and France fought Austria; after a brief war the Austrians were left with

only Venetia in Italy. Cavour now set to work to incorporate other Italian states into Sardinia, a part of the price being that Sardinian Savoy had to be given to France. Cavour died in 1861, and debate still continues over what was the extent of his real aims, but by 1871 his successors had produced a united Italy under the former king of Sardinia, who was thus recompensed for the loss of Savoy, the ancestral duchy of his house. In that year Germany was united, too. Bismarck had begun by rallying German liberal sentiment to the Prussian cause once again in a nasty little war against Denmark in 1864. Two years later Prussia defeated Austria in a lightning campaign in Bohemia, thus at last ending the Hohenzollern-Habsburg duel for supremacy in Germany begun in 1740 by Frederick II. The war which did this was rather a registration of an accomplished fact than its achievement, for since 1848 Austria had been much weakened in German affairs. In that year, German liberals

had offered a German crown, not to the emperor, but to the king of Prussia. Nevertheless, some states had still looked to Vienna for leadership and patronage, and they were now left alone to meet Prussian bullying. The Habsburg empire now became wholly Danubian and its foreign policy was preoccupied with south-east Europe and the Balkans. It had retired from the Netherlands in 1815, Venetia had been exacted by the Prussians for the Italians in 1866, and now it left Germany to its own devices, too. Immediately after the peace the Hungarians seized the opportunity to inflict a further defeat on the humiliated monarchy by obtaining a virtual autonomy for the half of the Habsburg monarchy made up of the lands of the Hungarian Crown. The empire thus became, in 1867, the Dual or Austro-Hungarian monarchy, divided rather untidily into two halves linked by little more than the dynasty itself and the conduct of a common foreign policy.

A contemporary painting depicts the triumphal entry of Victor Emmanuel II of Sardinia, Piedmont and Savoy and Napoleon III into Milan on 8 June, 1859. Count Cavour's influence on plebiscites held in 1860 resulted in the incorporation of Parma, Modena, Romagna and Tuscany into the Italian union, under the crown of Victor Emmanuel II.

Giuseppe Garibaldi (1807–1882), the liberator of Sicily and Naples, was one of the heroes of the Italian Risorgimento nationalist movement. His triumphal entry into Naples in 1860, pictured here, had Cavour's tacit support.

THE PRUSSIAN SECOND REICH

German unification required one further step. It had gradually dawned on France that the assertion of Prussian power beyond the Rhine was not in the French interest; instead of a disputed Germany, she now faced one dominated by one important military power. The Richelieu era had crumbled away unnoticed. Bismarck used this new awareness, together with Napoleon III's weaknesses at home and international isolation, to provoke France into a foolish declaration of war in 1870. Victory in this war set the coping-stone on the new edifice of German nationality, for Prussia had taken the lead in "defending" Germany against France – and there were still Germans alive who could remember what French armies had done in Germany under an earlier Napoleon. The Prussian army destroyed the Second Empire in France (it was to be the last monarchical régime in that country) and created the German Empire, the Second

Reich, as it was called, to distinguish it from the medieval empire. In practice, it was a Prussian domination cloaked in federal forms, but as a German national state it satisfied many German liberals. It was dramatically and appropriately founded in 1871 when the king of Prussia accepted the crown of united Germany (which his predecessor had refused to take from German liberals in 1848) from his fellow-princes in the palace of Louis XIV at Versailles.

REVOLUTIONARY TENDENCIES BEGIN TO WANE

There had been in fifty years a revolution in international affairs and it would have consequences for world, as well as European, history. Germany had replaced France as the dominant land-power in Europe as France had replaced Spain in the seventeenth century. This fact was to overshadow Europe's international relations until they ceased to be determined by forces originating within her. It owed just a little to revolutionary politics in the narrow and strict sense. The conscious revolutionaries of the nineteenth century had achieved nothing comparable with the work of Cavour, Bismarck and, half in spite of himself, Napoleon III. This is very odd, given the hopes entertained of revolution in this period, and the fears felt for it. Revolution had achieved little except at the fringes of Europe and had even begun to show signs of flagging. Down to 1848 there had been plenty of revolutions, to say nothing of plots, conspiracies and *pronunciamientos* which did not justify the name. After 1848 there were very few. Another Polish revolution took place in 1863, but this was the only outbreak of note in the lands of the great powers until 1871.

An ebbing of revolutionary effort by then is understandable. Revolutions seemed to

William I (1797–1888), King of Prussia, is proclaimed Emperor of Germany at Versailles on 18 January, 1871.

have achieved little outside France and had there brought disillusion and dictatorship. Some of their goals were being achieved in other ways. Cavour and his followers had created a united Italy, after all, greatly to the chagrin of Mazzini, since it was not one of which that revolutionary could approve, and Bismarck had done what many of the German liberals of 1848 had hoped for by providing a Germany which was indisputably a great power. Other ends were being achieved by economic progress; for all the horrors of the poverty which it contained, nineteenth-century Europe was getting richer and was giving more and more of its peoples a larger share of its wealth. Even quite short-term factors helped here. The year 1848 was soon followed by the great gold discoveries of California which provided a flow of bullion to stimulate the world economy in the 1850s and 1860s; confidence grew and unemployment fell in these decades and this was good for social peace.

THE GROWING POWER OF CENTRAL GOVERNMENT

A more fundamental reason why revolutions were less frequent was, perhaps, that they became more difficult to carry out. Governments were finding it steadily easier to grapple with them, largely for technical reasons. The nineteenth century created modern police forces. Better communications by rail and telegraph gave new power to central government in dealing with distant revolt. Above all, armies had a growing technical superiority to rebellion. As early as 1795 a French government showed that once it had control of the regular armed forces, and was prepared to use them, it could master Paris. During the long peace from 1815 to 1848 many European armies in fact became much more instruments of security, directed potentially against their own populations, than means of international competition, directed against foreign enemies. It was only the

The unification process in 19th-century Germany: some milestones

1806 The organization of The Confederation of the Rhine (12 July) of 16 princes under French domination. Francis II gives up the title of Holy Roman Emperor (6 August).

1815 The creation by the Treaty of Vienna of the Germanic Confederation of 38 sovereign powers.

1819 Prussia establishes a uniform tariff for all her territories and signs a tariff agreement with Schwarzburg-Sonderhausen (October). The beginning of the Zollverein (Customs Union).

1844 The Zollverein now includes most states of the Germanic Confederation but not Austria.

1848 In the wake of the revolutionary "March Days", the king of Prussia promises that Prussia will be "merged into Germany". The Frankfurt National Assembly, the first all-Germany parliament elected by democratic suffrage, meets on 18 May.

1849 The Frankfurt National Assembly adopts a constitution and elects the king of Prussia "Emperor of the Germans" (28 March), but he refuses the crown.

1850 The old Germanic Confederation is re-established.

1852 Hanover, Brunswick and Mecklenburg join the Zollverein (all non-Austrian German states are now members).

1863–1865 A crisis over the Danish claims to Schleswig-Holstein leaves Prussia, not Austria, as the focus of German nationalist hopes.

1866 Prussia engineers war with Austria and declares the Germanic Confederation at an end. After victory at Sadowa (3 July, Königgrätz), peace is made (Treaty of Prague, 23 August).

1867 Treaties between Prussia and German states north of the river Main lead to the North German Confederation, a federal structure dominated by Prussia. The Zollparlament is set up on 8 July, including representation of four South German states as well as the North German Reichstag (parliament) to deal with customs questions.

1870 France declares war on Prussia (19 July), which receives support of South German states. Decisive French defeat at Sedan (1 September).

1871 William I of Prussia is proclaimed German Emperor at Versailles after negotiation with all the German states, North and South. The new, federal, empire consists of 25 states, with a common Reichstag.

defection of important sections of the armed forces which permitted successful revolution in Paris in 1830 and 1848; once such forces were available to the government, battles like that of the June Days of 1848 (which one observer called the greatest slave-war in history) could only end with the defeat of the rebels. From that year, indeed, no popular revolution was ever to succeed in a major European country against a government whose control of its armed forces was unshaken by defeat in war or by subversion, and which was determined to use its power.

THE PARIS COMMUNE

The power of an effective army was vividly and bloodily demonstrated in 1871, when a rebellious Paris was once again crushed by a French government in little more than a week with a toll of dead as great as that exacted by the Terror of 1793–4. A popular régime which drew to itself a wide range of radicals and reformers set itself up in the capital as the "Commune" of Paris, a name evocative of traditions of municipal independence going back to the Middle Ages and, more

This French drawing entitled *Le Mur des Fédérés* shows the execution of communards on 28 May, 1871, the day after the fall of the Paris Commune.

important, to 1793, when the Commune (or city council) of Paris had been the centre of revolutionary fervour. The Commune of 1871 was able to take power because in the aftermath of defeat by the Germans the government could not disarm the capital of the weapons with which it had successfully withstood a siege, and because the same defeat had inflamed many Parisians against the government they believed to have let them down. During its brief life (there were a few weeks of quiet while the government prepared its riposte) the Commune did very little, but it produced a lot of left-wing rhetoric and was soon seen as the embodiment of social revolution. This gave additional bitterness to the efforts to suppress it. They came when the government had reassembled its forces from returning prisoners of war to reconquer Paris, which became the scene of brief but bloody street-fighting. Once again, regularly constituted armed forces overcame workmen and shopkeepers manning hastily improvised barricades.

If anything could do so, the ghastly failure of the Paris Commune should have killed the revolutionary myth, both in its power to terrify and its power to inspire. Yet it did not. If anything, it strengthened it.

SOCIALISM

CONSERVATIVES FOUND IT a great standby to have the Commune example to hand in evoking the dangers lurking always ready to burst out from under the surface of society. Revolutionaries had a new episode of heroism and martyrdom to add to an apostolic succession of revolutionaries running already from 1789 to 1848. But the Commune also revivified the revolutionary mythology because of a new factor whose importance had already struck both Left and

This portrayal of early rail travel by the French artist Honoré Daumier (1808–1878) is entitled *The Third Class Carriage*.

Right. This was socialism.

This word (like its relative, "socialist") has come to cover a great many different things, and did so almost from the start. Both words were first commonly used in France round about 1830 to describe theories and men opposed to a society run on market principles and to an economy operated on laissez-faire lines, of which the main beneficiaries (they thought) were the wealthy. Economic and social egalitarianism is fundamental to the socialist idea. Most socialists have been able to agree on that. They have usually believed that in a good society there would be no classes oppressing one another through the advantages given to one by the ownership of wealth. All socialists, too, could agree that there was nothing sacred about property, whose rights buttressed injustice; some sought its complete abolition and were called communists. "Property is theft" was one very successful slogan.

SOCIALIST THOUGHT

Such ideas might be frightening, but were not very novel. Egalitarian ideas have fascinated human beings throughout history and the Christian rulers of Europe had managed without difficulty to reconcile social arrangements resting on sharp contrasts of wealth with the practice of a religion one of whose greatest hymns praised God for filling the hungry with good things and sending the rich empty away. What happened in the early nineteenth century was that such ideas seemed to become at once more dangerous and more widespread. There was also a need for new terms because of other developments. One was that the success of liberal political reform appeared to show that legal equality was not enough, if it was deprived of content by dependence on others' economic power, or denatured by poverty and attendant ignorance. Another was that already in the

The more wealthy passengers enjoyed considerable luxury on the new trains, as this 19th-century English painting, entitled *Travelling in First Class*, demonstrates.

eighteenth century a few thinkers had seen big discrepancies of wealth as irrationalities in a world which could and should (they thought) be regulated to produce the greatest good of the greatest number. In the French Revolution some thinkers and agitators already pressed forward demands in which later generations would see socialist ideas. Egalitarian ideas none the less only became socialism in a modern sense when they began to grapple with the problems of the new epoch of economic and social change, above all with those presented by industrialization.

This often required a great perspicacity, for these changes were very slow in making their impact outside Great Britain and Belgium, the first continental country to be industrialized in the same degree. Yet perhaps because the contrast they presented with traditional society was so stark, even the small beginnings of concentration in capitalist finance and manufacturing were remarked.

One of the first men to grasp their potentially very great implications for social organization was a French nobleman, Claude Saint-Simon. His seminal contribution to socialist thought was to consider the impact on society of technological and scientific advance. Saint-Simon thought that they not only made planned organization of the economy imperative, but implied (indeed, demanded) the replacement of the traditional ruling classes, aristocratic and rural in their outlook, by élites representing new economic and intellectual forces. Such ideas influenced many thinkers (most of them French) who in the 1830s advocated greater egalitarianism; they seemed to show that on rational as well as ethical grounds such change was desirable. Their doctrines made enough impact and considerations were enough talked about to terrify the French possessing classes in 1848, who thought they saw in the June Days a "socialist" revolution. Socialists willingly identified themselves for the most part with the tradition of the French Revolution, picturing the realization of their ideals as its next phase, so the misinterpretation is understandable.

THE COMMUNIST MANIFESTO

In 1848, at this juncture, there appeared a pamphlet which is the most important document in the history of socialism. It is always known as *The Communist Manifesto* (though this was not the title under which it appeared). It was largely the work of a young German Jew, Karl Marx, and with it the point is reached at which the prehistory of socialism can be separated from its history. Marx proclaimed a complete break with what he called the "utopian socialism" of his predecessors. Utopian socialists attacked industrial capitalism because they thought it was unjust; Marx thought this beside the point. Nothing, according to Marx, could be hoped for from

The socialist thinker Count Claude de Saint-Simon (1760–1825) is often cited as the founder of French socialism.

arguments to persuade people that change was morally desirable. Everything depended on the way history was going, towards the actual and inevitable creation of a new working class by industrial society, the rootless wage-earners of the new industrial cities which he termed the industrial proletariat. This class was bound, according to him, to act in a revolutionary way. History was working upon them so as to generate revolutionary capacity and mentality. It would present them with conditions to which revolution was the only logical outcome and that revolution would be, by those conditions, guaranteed success. What mattered was not that capitalism was morally wrong, but that it was already out-of-date and therefore historically doomed. Marx asserted that every society had a particular system of property rights and class relationships, and these accordingly shaped its particular political arrangements. Politics were bound to express economic forces. They would change as the particular organization of society changed under the influence of economic developments, and therefore, sooner or later (and Marx seems to have thought sooner), the revolution would sweep away capitalist society and its forms as capitalist society had already swept away feudal.

A SECULAR RELIGION

There was much more to Marx than the theory of historical inevitability, but this was a striking and encouraging message which gave him domination of the international socialist movement which emerged in the next twenty years. The assurance that history was

Karl Marx (1818–1883) is depicted in his study in this 19th-century drawing.

on their side was a great tonic to revolutionaries. They learnt with gratitude that the cause to which they were impelled anyway by motives ranging from a sense of injustice to the promptings of envy was predestined to triumph. This was essentially a religious faith. For all its intellectual possibilities as an analytical instrument, Marxism came to be above all a popular mythology, resting on a view of history which said that human beings were bound by necessity because their institutions were determined by the evolving methods of production, and on a faith that the working class were the Chosen People whose pilgrimage through a wicked world would end in the triumphal establishment of a just society in which necessity's iron law would cease to operate. Social revolutionaries could thus feel confident of scientifically irrefutable arguments for irresistible progress towards the socialist millennium while clinging to a revolutionary activism it seemed to make unnecessary. Marx himself seems to have followed his teaching more cautiously, applying it only to the broad, sweeping changes in history which individuals are powerless to resist and not to its detailed unfolding. Perhaps it is not surprising that, like many masters, he did not recognize all his pupils: he came later to protest that he was not a Marxist.

MARXIST MOVEMENTS

This new religion was an inspiration to working-class organization. Trades unions and cooperatives already existed in some countries; the First International organization of working men appeared in 1863. Though it included many who did not subscribe to Marx's views (anarchists, among others), his influence was paramount within it (he was its secretary). Its name frightened conservatives,

some of whom blamed the Paris Commune on it. Whatever their justification, their instincts were right. What happened in the years after 1848 was that socialism captured the revolutionary tradition from the liberals, and a belief in the historical role of an industrial working class still barely visible outside England (let alone predominant in most countries) was tacked on to the tradition which held that, broadly speaking, revolution could not be wrong. Forms of thinking about politics evolved in the French Revolution were thus transferred to societies to which they would prove increasingly inappropriate. How easy such a transition could be was shown by the way Marx snapped up the drama and mythical exaltation of the Paris Commune for

Bakunin *versus* Marx

"Marx is an authoritarian, centralist communist. He wants what we want: the triumph of economic and social equality, but through the State and by the power of the State; by the dictatorship of a powerful and, one could say, despotic provisional government, that is to say, denying liberty. His economic ideal is that of a State converted into the sole owner of all land and all capital, cultivating the former through agricultural associations, well-remunerated and managed by its civil engineers, and collectivizing the latter through industrial and commercial associations.

"We want that same triumph of economic and social equality to come through the abolition of the State and everything known as Legal Rights, which, in our view, is the permanent negation of human rights. We want to rebuild society and to build human unity, not from top to bottom with the aid of any authorities, but from bottom to top, through the free federation of all types of workmen's associations, freed from the yoke of the State."

An extract from a private letter written in 1872 by Russian anarchist Mikhail Bakunin (1814–1876).

socialism. In a powerful tract he annexed it to his own theories, though it was, in fact, the product of many complicated and differing forces and expressed very little in the way of egalitarianism, let alone "scientific" socialism. It emerged, moreover, in a city which, though huge, was not one of the great manufacturing centres in which he predicted proletarian revolution would mature. These remained, instead, stubbornly quiescent. The Commune was, in fact, the last and greatest example of revolutionary and traditional Parisian radicalism. It was a great failure (and socialism suffered from it, too, because of the repressive measures it provoked), yet Marx made it central to socialist mythology.

NICHOLAS I OF RUSSIA

RUSSIA SEEMED, except in her Polish lands, immune to the disturbances troubling other continental great powers. The French Revolution had been another of those experi-

Byron on the tsar of Russia

Referring to the tsar of Russia's interference in Greece's struggle for independence from the Ottoman Empire, Byron wrote:

"The aid evaded, and the cold delay,
Prolong'd but in the hope to make a prey;–
These, these shall tell the tale, and Greece can show
The false friend is worse than the infuriate foe.
But this is well: Greeks only should free Greece,
Not the barbarian, with his mask of peace.
How should the autocrat of bondage be
The king of serfs, and set the nations free?
Better still serve the haughty Mussulman,
Than swell the Cossaque's prowling caravan ...
Better still toil for masters, than await,
The slave of slaves, before a Russian gate,–
Number'd by hordes, a human capital,
A live estate, existing but for thrall,
Lotted by thousands, as a meet reward
For the first courtier in the Czar's regard;
While their immediate owner never tastes
His sleep, *sans* dreaming of Siberia's wastes:
Better succumb even to their own despair,
And drive the camel than purvey the bear."

An extract from v. 6 of *The Age of Bronze* by Lord Byron, 1823.

The domestic policy of Nicholas I (1796–1855), portrayed here, reflected that of his ancestors: despotism propped up by the power of the military. His pan-Slavism – he aimed to Russify all the peoples of his empire – led to Roman Catholics and Protestants being encouraged to become part of the Russian Orthodox Church.

ences which, like feudalism, Renaissance or Reformation, decisively shaped Western Europe and passed Russia by. Although Alexander I, the tsar under whom Russia met the 1812 invasion, had indulged himself with liberal ideas and had even thought of a constitution, nothing seemed to come of this. A formal liberalization of Russian institutions did not begin until the 1860s, and even then its source was not revolutionary contagion. It is true that liberalism and revolutionary ideologies did not quite leave Russia untouched before this. Alexander's reign had seen something of an opening of a Pandora's box of ideas and it had thrown up a small group of

critics of the régime who found their models in Western Europe. Some of the Russian officers who went there with the armies which pursued Napoleon to Paris were led by what they saw and heard to make unfavourable comparisons with their homeland; this was the beginning of Russian political opposition. In an autocracy opposition was bound to mean conspiracy. Some of them took part in the organization of secret societies which attempted a coup amid the uncertainty caused by the death of Alexander in 1825; this was called the "Decembrist" movement. It collapsed but only after giving a fright to Nicholas I, a tsar who decisively and negatively affected Russia's historical destiny at a crucial moment by ruthlessly turning on political liberalism and seeking to crush it. In

part because of the immobility which he imposed upon her, Nicholas' reign influenced Russia's destiny more than any since that of Peter the Great. A dedicated believer in autocracy, he confirmed the Russian tradition of authoritarian bureaucracy, the management of cultural life, and the rule of the secret police just when the other great conservative powers were, however unwillingly, beginning to move in the opposite direction. There was, of course, much to build on already in the historical legacies which differentiated Russian autocracy from Western European monarchy. But there were also great challenges to be met and Nicholas' reign was a response to these as well as a simple deployment of the old methods of despotism by a man determined to use them.

Moscow is depicted by Fiodor Alexeyev in 1811, during the reign of Tsar Alexander I (1777–1825).

The Russian nobility became ever more Europeanized during the 19th century. The intelligentsia began to identify with German idealism, utopian French socialism and Romanticism. Here, intellectuals are shown taking tea in a St Petersburg salon in 1830.

The Russian nobility became ever more Europeanized during the 19th century. The intelligentsia began to identify with German idealism, utopian French socialism and Romanticism. Here, intellectuals are shown taking tea in a St Petersburg salon in 1830.

OFFICIAL IDEOLOGY

The ethnic, linguistic and geographical diversity of the empire had begun to pose problems far outrunning the capacity of Muscovite tradition to deal with them. The population of the empire itself more than doubled in the forty years after 1770. This ever-diversifying society none the less remained overwhelmingly backward; its few cities were hardly a part of the vast rural expanses in which they stood and often seemed insubstantial and impermanent, more like temporary though huge encampments than settled centres of civilization. The greatest expansion had been to the south and south-east; here new élites had to be incorporated in the imperial structure and to stress the religious ties between the Orthodox was one of the easiest ways to do this. As the conflict with Napoleon had compromised the old prestige of things French and the sceptical ideas of the Enlightenment associated with that country, a new emphasis was now given to religion in the evolution of a new ideological basis for the Russian Empire under Nicholas. "Official Nationality", as it was called, was Slavophile and religious in doctrine, bureaucratic in form and gave Russia an ideological unity it had lost since outgrowing its historic centre in Muscovy.

The importance of official ideology was from this time one of the great differences between Russia and Western Europe. Until the last decade of the twentieth century Russian governments never gave up their belief in official ideology as a unifying force. Yet this did not mean that daily life in the middle of the century, either for the civilized classes or the mass of a backward population, was much different from that of other parts of Eastern and Central Europe. Yet Russian intellectuals argued about whether Russia was or was not a European country, and this is not surprising; Russia's roots were different from those of countries further west. What is more, a decisive turn was taken under Nicholas, from the beginning of whose reign possibilities of change which were at least being felt in other dynastic states in the first half of the nineteenth century were simply not allowed to appear in Russia. It was the land *par excellence* of censorship and police. In the long run this was bound to exclude certain possibilities of modernization (though other obstacles rooted in Russian society seem equally important), but in the short run it was highly successful. Russia passed through the whole nineteenth century without revolution; revolts in Russian Poland in 1830–31 and 1863–4 were ruthlessly suppressed, the more easily because Poles and Russians cherished traditions of mutual dislike.

RUSSIAN EXPANSION

The other side of the coin was the almost continuous violence and disorder of a savage and primitive rural society, and a mounting and more and more violent tradition of conspiracy which perhaps incapacitated Russia even further for normal politics and the shared assumptions they required. Unfriendly

Pushkin describes St Petersburg

"I love you, Peter's own creation;
I love your stern, your stately air,
Nevá's majestical pulsation,
the granite that her quaysides wear,
your railings with their iron shimmer,
your pensive nights in the half-gloom,
translucent twilight, moonless glimmer,
when, sitting lampless in my room,
I write and read; when, faintly shining,
the streets in their immense outlining
are empty, given up to dreams;
when Admiralty's needle gleams;
when not admitting shades infernal
into the golden sky, one glow
succeeds another, and nocturnal
tenure has one half-hour to go;
I love your brutal winter, freezing
the air to so much windless space;
by broad Nevá the sledges breezing;
brighter than roses each girl's face; ...
... I love it when some warlike duty
livens the Field of Mars, and horse
and foot impose on that concourse
their monolithic brand of beauty;
above the smooth-swaying vanguard
victorious, tattered flags are streaming,
on brazen helmets light is gleaming,
helmets that war has pierced and scarred.
I love the martial detonation,
the citadel in smoke and roar,
when the North's Empress to the nation
has given a son for empire, or
when there's some new triumph in war
victorious Russia's celebrating;
or when Nevá breaks the blue ice,
sweeps it to seaward, slice on slice,
and smells that days of spring are waiting.
    "Metropolis of Peter, stand,
steadfast as Russia, stand in splendour!
Even the elements by your hand
have been subdued and made surrender;
let Finland's waves forget the band
of hate and bondage down the ages,
nor trouble with their fruitless rages
Peter the Great's eternal sleep!"

Extract from *The Bronze Horseman* by Alexander Pushkin, 1833, translated by Charles Johnston.

critics variously described Nicholas' reign as an ice age, a plague zone and a prison, but not for the last time in Russian history the preservation of a harsh and unyielding despotism at home was not incompatible with a strong international role. This rested upon Russia's huge military superiority. When armies contended with muzzle-loaders and no important technological differences distinguished one from another her vast numbers were decisive. On Russian military strength rested the anti-revolutionary international security system, as 1849 showed. But Russian foreign policy had other successes, too. Pressure was consistently kept up on the central Asian khanates and on China. The left bank of the Amur became Russian and in 1860 Vladivostok was founded. Great concessions were exacted from Persia and during the nineteenth century Russia absorbed Georgia and a part of Armenia. For a time there was even a determined effort to pursue

Russian expansion in North America, where there were forts in Alaska and settlements in northern California until the 1840s.

The major effort of Russian foreign policy, nevertheless, was directed to the south-west, towards Ottoman Europe. Wars in 1806–12 and 1828 carried the Russian frontier across Bessarabia to the Pruth and the mouth of the Danube. It was by now clear that the partition of the Ottoman Empire in Europe would be as central to nineteenth-century diplomacy as the partition of Poland had been to that of the eighteenth, but there was an important difference: the interests of more powers were involved this time and the complicating factor of national sentiment among the subject peoples of the Ottoman Empire would make an agreed outcome much more difficult. As it happened, the Ottoman Empire survived far longer than might have been expected, and an eastern question is still bothering statesmen.

The railway at Balaklava is depicted in this English illustration of the port after its capture from the Russians during the Crimean War.

A PERIOD OF CHANGE IN IMPERIAL RUSSIA

Some of the complicating factors of the Eastern Question led to the Crimean War, which began with a Russian occupation of Ottoman provinces on the lower Danube. In Russia's internal affairs the war was more important than in those of any other country. It revealed that the military colossus of the 1815 restoration now no longer enjoyed an unquestioned superiority. She was defeated on her own territory and obliged to accept a peace which involved the renunciation for the foreseeable future of her traditional goals in the Black Sea area. Fortunately, in the middle of the war Nicholas I had died. This simplified the problems of his successor; defeat meant that change had to come. Some modernization of Russian institutions was unavoidable

if Russia was again to generate a power commensurate with her vast potential, which had become unrealizable within her traditional framework. When the Crimean War broke out there was still no Russian railway south of Moscow. Russia's once important contribution to European industrial production had hardly grown since 1800 and was now far outstripped by others'. Her agriculture remained one of the least productive in the world and yet her population steadily rose, pressing harder upon its resources. It was in these circumstances that Russia at last underwent radical change. Though less dramatic than many upheavals in the rest of Europe it was in fact more of a revolution than much that went by that name elsewhere, for what was at last uprooted was the institution which lay at the very roots of Russian life, serfdom.

The Orthodox Church played a central role in the lives of the vast majority of Russia's rural population in the 19th century. Here, a painting of 1878 depicts the arrival of an icon in a Russian village.

Russian peasants are shown tilling the soil in spring in this scene dating from 1820–1830.

THE EMANCIPATION OF THE SERFS

Its extension had been the leading characteristic of Russian social history since the seventeenth century. Even Nicholas had agreed that it was the central evil of Russian society. His reign had been marked by increasingly frequent serf insurrections, attacks on landlords, crop-burning and cattle-maiming. The refusal of dues was almost the least alarming form of popular resistance to it. Yet it was appallingly difficult for the rider to get off the elephant. The vast majority of Russians were serfs. They could not be transformed overnight by mere legislation into wage labourers or smallholders, nor could the state accept the administrative burden which would suddenly be thrown upon it if the services discharged by the manorial system should be withdrawn and nothing put in their place. Nicholas had not dared to proceed. Alexander II did. After years of study of the evidence and possible advantages and disadvantages of different forms of abolition, the tsar issued in 1861 the edict which marked an epoch in Russian history and won him the title of the "Tsar Liberator". The one card Russian government could play was the unquestioned authority of the autocrat and it was now put to good use.

The edict gave the serfs personal freedom and ended bond labour. It also gave them allotments of land. But these were to be paid for by redemption charges whose purpose was to make the change acceptable to the landowners. To secure the repayments and offset the dangers of suddenly introducing a

Russian canal workers tow barges along the River Volga in the 1870s in a scene by the great Russian naturalist painter Ilya Repin (1844–1930).

free labour market, peasants remained to a considerable degree subject to the authority of their village community, which was given the charge of distributing the land allotments on a family basis.

It would not be long before a great deal would be heard about the shortcomings of this settlement. Yet there is much to be said for it and in retrospect it seems a massive achievement. A few years later the United States would emancipate its black slaves. There were far fewer of them than there were Russian peasants and they lived in a country of much greater economic opportunity, yet the effect of throwing them on the labour market, exposed to the pure theory of laissez-faire economic liberalism, was to exacerbate a problem with whose ultimate consequences the United States is still grappling. In Russia the largest measure of social engineering in

recorded history down to this time was carried out without comparable dislocation and it opened the way to modernization for what was potentially one of the strongest powers on earth. It was the indispensable first step towards making the peasant look beyond the estate for available industrial employment.

REFORM

More immediately, liberation opened an era of reform; there followed other measures which by 1870 gave Russia a representative system of local government and a reformed judiciary. When, in 1871, the Russians took advantage of the Franco-Prussian War to denounce some of the restrictions placed on their freedom in the Black Sea in 1856, there

A religious procession takes place in Kursk province c.1880, portrayed by Ilya Repin.

was almost a symbolic warning to Europe in what they did. After tackling her greatest problem and beginning to modernize her institutions Russia was again announcing that she would after all be master in her own house. The resumption of the most consistently and long-pursued policies of expansion in modern history was only a matter of time.

A Russian nobleman with some of his serfs is somewhat sentimentally depicted in a French publication of 1861.

5 POLITICAL CHANGE: THE ANGLO-SAXON WORLD

Painted by Ford Madox Brown in 1855, *The Last Farewell to England* conveys something of both the sadness and the hope of emigrants leaving Europe for the New World.

No EUROPEAN NATION has so successfully seeded the globe with its own stocks as the United Kingdom. By the end of the nineteenth century it had created an Anglo-Saxon world which was an identifiable sub-unit within the ambit of European civilization, with an historical destiny diverging from that of the European continent. Its components included growing British communities in Canada, Australia, New Zealand and South Africa (the first and last containing other important national elements, too). At the heart of this world were

the two great Atlantic nations, one the greatest world power of the nineteenth century, one that of the next.

BRITAIN AND THE UNITED STATES: SIMILARITIES

THE TWO ATLANTIC NATIONS were at first sight so different – and so many people found it profitable to keep on pointing it out – that it is easy to overlook how much the United Kingdom and the young United States of America had in common for much of the nineteenth century. Though one was a monarchy and the other a republic, both countries escaped first the absolutist and then the revolutionary currents of continental Europe. Anglo-Saxon politics, of course, changed quite as radically as those of any other countries in the nineteenth century. But they were not transformed by the same political forces as those of continental states nor in the same way.

Their similarity arose in part because the two countries shared more than they usually admitted. One aspect of their curious relations was that the United States could still without a sense of paradox call England the mother country. The heritage of English culture and language was for a long time paramount in the United States; immigration from other European countries only became overwhelming in the second half of the nineteenth century. Though by the middle of the century many Americans – perhaps most – already had the blood of other European nations in their veins, the tone of society was

Broadway in New York City is shown in an anonymous engraving from 1840. By that date, New York was the most highly populated state in the USA and its principal city had become the nation's most important trade, transport and industrial centre.

long set by those of British stock. It was not until 1837 that there was a president who did not have an English, Scotch, or Irish surname (the next would not be until 1901, and there have been only four down to the present day).

COMMERCE AND MUTUAL FASCINATION

Post-colonial problems made, as they did in far later times, for emotional, sometimes violent, and always complex relations between the United States and the United Kingdom. But they were also much more than this. They were, for example, shot through with economic connexions. Far from dwindling (as had been feared) after independence, commerce between the two countries had gone on from strength to strength. English capitalists found the United States an attractive place for investment even after repeated and unhappy experiences with the bonds of defaulting

states. British money was heavily invested in American railroads, banking, and insurance. Meanwhile the ruling élites of the two countries were at once fascinated and repelled by each other. The English commented acidly on the vulgarity and rawness of American life but warmed as if by instinct to its energy, optimism and opportunity; Americans found it hard to come to terms with monarchy and hereditary titles but sought to penetrate the fascinating mysteries of English culture and society no less eagerly for that.

PHYSICAL ISOLATION

More striking than the huge differences between them was what the United Kingdom and the United States had in common when considered from the standpoint of continental Europe. Above all, both were able to combine liberal and democratic politics with spectacular advances in wealth and power. They did

Transatlantic trade was crucial to the growth of the United States' economy. The *Great Western* transatlantic steamship is seen departing from Bristol in Rhode Island in 1850.

this in very different circumstances, but at least one was common to both, the fact of isolation: Great Britain had the Channel between herself and Europe, the United States had the Atlantic Ocean. This physical remoteness long masked from Europeans the international potential of the young republic and the huge opportunities facing it in the West. At the peace of 1783 the British had defended the Americans' frontier interests in such a way that there inevitably lay ahead a period of expansion for the United States; what was not clear was how far it might carry nor what other powers it might involve. This was in part a matter of geographical ignorance. No one knew for certain what the western half of the continent might contain. For decades the huge spaces just across the eastern mountain ranges would provide a big enough field of expansion. In 1800 the United States was still psychologically and actually very much a matter of the Atlantic seaboard and the Ohio valley.

AMERICAN DIPLOMATIC ISOLATION

The United States' political frontiers were then ill-defined, but imposed relations with France, Spain and the United Kingdom. None the less, if frontier questions could be settled, then a practical isolation might be attained, for the only other interests which might involve Americans in the affairs of other countries were, on the one hand, trade and the protection of her nationals, and, on the other, foreign intervention in the affairs of the United States. The French Revolution appeared briefly to pose the chance of the latter, and caused a quarrel, but for the most part it was frontiers and trade which preoccupied American diplomacy under the young republic. Both also aroused powerful and often divisive or potentially divisive forces in domestic politics.

The American aspiration to non-involvement with the outside world was already clear in 1793, when the troubles of the French revolutionary war led to a Neutrality Proclamation rendering American citizens liable to prosecution in American courts if they took any part in the Anglo-French war. The bias of American policy already expressed in this received its classical formulation in 1796. In the course of Washington's Farewell Address to his "Friends and Fellow-Citizens" as his second term as president drew to a close, he chose to comment on the objectives and methods which a successful republican foreign policy should embody, in language to be deeply influential both on later American statesmen and on the national psychology. In retrospect, what is now especially striking about Washington's thoughts is their predominantly negative and passive tone. "The great rule of conduct for us," he began, "in regard to foreign nations is, in extending our commercial relations, to have with them as little political connection as possible." "Europe has a set of primary interests," he continued, "which to us have none, or a very remote relation ... Our detached and distant situation invites and enables us to pursue a different course ... It is our true policy to steer clear of permanent alliances with any portion of the foreign world." Moreover, Washington also warned Americans against assumptions of permanent or special hostility or friendship with any other nation. In all this there was no hint of America's future destiny as a world power (Washington did not even consider other than European relations; America's future Pacific and Asian role was inconceivable in 1796).

WAR WITH BRITAIN

By and large, a pragmatic approach, case by case, to the foreign relations of the young republic was indeed the policy pursued by Washington's successors in the presidency. There was only one war with another great power, that between the United States and Great Britain in 1812. Besides contributing to the growth of nationalist feeling in the young republic, the struggle led both to the appearance of Uncle Sam as the caricature embodiment of the nation and to the composition of the "Star-spangled Banner". More importantly, it marked an important stage in the evolving relations of the two countries. Officially, British interference with trade during the struggle with the Napoleonic blockade had caused the American declaration of war, but more important had been the hopes of some Americans that the conquest of Canada would follow. It did not, and the failure of military expansion did much to determine that the future negotiation of the boundary problems with the British should be by peaceful negotiation. Though Anglophobia had been aroused again in the United States by the war, the fighting (which had its humiliations for both sides) cleared the air. In future boundary disputes it was tacitly understood that neither American nor British governments were willing to consider war except under extreme provocation. In this setting the northern boundary of the

Because news of the peace treaty of Ghent, signed on 28 December, 1814, was slow to reach the battlefield, General Jackson took on the British army at New Orleans on 8 January, 1815. Jackson's use of earthworks and cotton bales as barricades was so effective that the battle lasted only half an hour. The defeated British army suffered more than 2,000 casualties and Jackson became a national hero.

United States was soon agreed as far west as the "Stony Mountains" (as the Rockies were then called); in 1845 it was carried further west to the sea and by then the disputed Maine boundary, too, had been agreed.

THE LOUISIANA PURCHASE

The greatest change in American territorial definition was brought about by the Louisiana Purchase. Roughly speaking, "Louisiana" was the area between the Mississippi and the Rockies. In 1803 it belonged, if somewhat theoretically, to the French, the Spanish having ceded it to them in 1800. This change had provoked American interest; if Napoleonic France envisaged a revival of French American empire, New Orleans, which controlled the mouth of the river down which so much American commerce already passed, was of vital importance. It was to buy freedom of navigation on the Mississippi that the United States entered a negotiation which ended with the purchase of an area larger than the then total area of the republic. On the modern map it includes Louisiana, Arkansas, Iowa, Nebraska, both the Dakotas, Minnesota west of the Mississippi, most of Kansas, Oklahoma, Montana, Wyoming and a big piece of Colorado. The price was $11,250,000.

This was the largest sale of land of all time and its consequences were appropriately huge. It transformed American domestic history. The opening of the way to the trans-Mississippi West was to lead to a shift in demographic and political balance of revolutionary import for the politics of the young republic. This shift was already showing itself in the second decade of the century when the population living west of the Alleghenies more than doubled. When the Purchase was rounded off by the acquisition of the Floridas from Spain, the United States had by 1819 legal sovereignty over territory bounded by the Atlantic and Gulf coasts from Maine to the Sabine river, the Red and Arkansas rivers, the Continental Divide and the line of the 49th Parallel agreed with the British.

A contemporary engraving depicts the port of New Orleans in the mid-19th century. The South's huge exports of raw cotton, tobacco and rice played a crucial role in the national economy of the United States.

The use of steam boats along the Mississippi and its tributaries from 1811 ensured safe, regular traffic linking the farming areas of the West and the Southern plantations to the markets in New Orleans. Water transport largely gave way to railways after the Civil War.

THE MONROE DOCTRINE

The United States was already the most important state in the Americas. Though there were still some European colonial possessions there, a major effort would be required to contest this fact, as the British had discovered in war. None the less, alarm about a possible European intervention in Latin America, together with Russian activity in the Pacific north-west, led to a clear American statement of the republic's determination to rule the roost in the western hemisphere. This was the "Monroe doctrine" of 1823, which said that no future European colonization in the hemisphere could be considered and that intervention by European powers in its affairs would be seen as unfriendly to the United States. As this suited British interests, the Monroe doctrine was easily maintained. It had the tacit underwriting of the Royal Navy and no European power could conceivably mount an American operation if British seapower was used against it.

The Monroe doctrine remains the bedrock of American hemisphere diplomacy to this day. One of its consequences was that other American nations would not be able to draw upon European support in defending

James Monroe (1758–1831) served as the fifth president of the USA between 1817 and 1825. His declaration, known as the Monroe doctrine, that further European colonization of the Americas would be seen as a direct threat to the United States, echoed a theme from Washington's farewell speech of 1796.

The emergence and consolidation of the USA

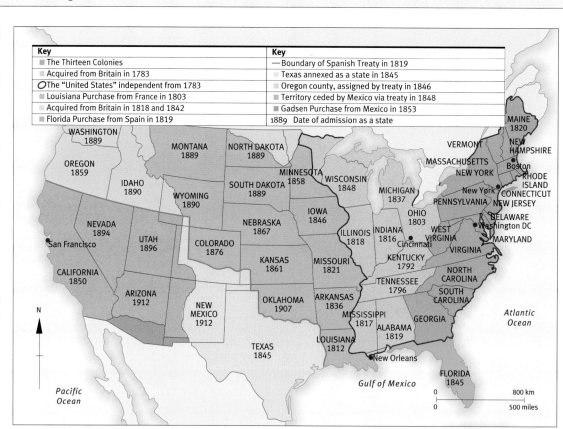

Key	
■ The Thirteen Colonies	— Boundary of Spanish Treaty in 1819
■ Acquired from Britain in 1783	Texas annexed as a state in 1845
○ The "United States" independent from 1783	Oregon county, assigned by treaty in 1846
■ Louisiana Purchase from France in 1803	■ Territory ceded by Mexico via treaty in 1848
■ Acquired from Britain in 1818 and 1842	■ Gadsen Purchase from Mexico in 1853
■ Florida Purchase from Spain in 1819	1889 Date of admission as a state

Between 1820 and 1860, the number of states rose from 23 to 33, and the population of the United States increased by 9.6 million to total 31.3 million inhabitants. There was continuous westward expansion during this period. The French territories in the Mississippi valley were purchased in 1803. Spanish territories were forcibly incorporated into the United States during the Florida campaign, in which annexation was disguised as purchase in 1819. The Oregon Treaty of 1846 fixed the 49th Parallel as the lower limit for the border with Canada. Texas, which had declared itself independent of Mexico, was annexed in 1845. After a successful war (1846–1848), the United States took New Mexico and California from Mexico. Large territories were taken from the Native North Americans through various treaties.

When a sufficient number of settlers requested it, a new acquisition became a territory; when it had more than 60,000 settlers, it could be formally recognized as a State and request admission to the Union.

their own independence against the United States. The main sufferer before 1860 was Mexico. American settlers within its borders rebelled and set up an independent Texan republic which was subsequently annexed by the United States. In the war that followed Mexico did very badly. The peace of 1848 stripped her, in consequence, of what would one day become Utah, Nevada, California and most of Arizona, an acquisition of territory which left only a small purchase of other Mexican land to be made to round off the mainland territory of the modern United States by 1853.

WESTWARD SETTLEMENT

In the seventy years after the Peace of Paris the republic expanded to fill half a continent.

Nearly four million people in 1790 had become nearly twenty-four million by 1850. Most of these still lived east of the Mississippi, it was true, and the only cities with more than 100,000 inhabitants were the three great Atlantic ports of Boston, New York and Philadelphia: none the less, the centre of gravity of the nation was moving westward. For a long time the political, commercial and cultural élites of the eastern seaboard would continue to dominate American society. But from the moment that the Ohio valley had been settled a western interest had been in existence; Washington's Farewell Address had already recognized its importance. The West was an increasingly decisive contributor to the politics of the next seventy years, until there came to a head the greatest crisis in the history of the United States and one which settled her destiny as a world power.

SLAVERY IN THE UNITED STATES

EXPANSION, both territorial and economic, shaped American history as profoundly as the democratic bias of her political institutions. Its influence on those institutions, too, was very great and sometimes glaring; sometimes they were transformed. Slavery is the outstanding example. When Washington began his presidency there were a little under 700,000 black slaves within the territories of the Union. This was a large number, but the framers of the constitution paid no special attention to them, except in so far as

Edgar Degas' famous painting depicts cotton trading in New Orleans in 1873. Around this time, falling cotton prices began to result in increased poverty in the South.

questions of political balance between the different states were involved. In the end it had been decided that a slave should count as three-fifths of a free man in deciding how many representatives each state should have.

Within the next half-century three things revolutionized this state of affairs. The first was an enormous extension of slavery. It was driven by a rapid increase in the world's consumption of cotton (above all in its consumption by the mills of England). This led to a doubling of the American crop in the 1820s and then its doubling again in the 1830s: by 1860, cotton provided two-thirds of the value of the total exports of the United States. This huge increase was obtained largely by cropping new land, and new plantations meant more labour. By 1820 there were already a million and a half black slaves, by 1860 about four million. In the Southern states slavery had become the foundation of the economic system. Because of this, Southern society became even more distinctive; it had always

been aware of the ways it differed from the more mercantile and urban northern states, but now its "peculiar institution", as slavery was called, came to be regarded by Southerners as the essential core of a particular civilization. By 1860 many of them thought of themselves as a nation, with a way of life they idealized and believed to be threatened by tyrannous interference from the outside. The expression and symbol of this interference was, in their view, the growing hostility of Congress to slavery.

THE EVOLUTION OF AMERICAN POLITICS

That slavery became a political issue was the second development changing its role in American life. It was part of a general evolution in American politics evident also in other ways. The early politics of the republic had reflected what were to be later called "sectional" interests and the Farewell Address itself had drawn attention to them. Roughly speaking, they produced political parties reflecting, on the one hand, mercantile and business interests which tended to look for strong federal government and protectionist legislation, and, on the other, agrarian and consumer interests which tended to assert the right of individual states and cheap money policies. At that stage slavery was hardly a political question; most political leaders seem to have thought of it as an evil which must succumb (though no one quite knew how) with the passage of time. This political world gradually gave way to a more modern one, partly as a result of the inherent tendencies of American institutions, partly because of social change. Judicial interpretation gave a strongly national and federal emphasis to the constitution. At the same time as congressional legislation was thus given new

The French political analyst Alexis de Tocqueville (1809–1859) produced a major study of the young United States, entitled *Democracy in America*, in 1835.

Democracy in America

"I don't think there is any country in the world where, proportionately, there are fewer ignorant people nor fewer wise people than in America. Primary education is available for everyone; higher education, for practically nobody … . Americans cannot spend more than the first few years of their lives on the general education of their intelligence. At fifteen, they start to work. Thus, their education tends to finish just at the moment when ours begins. If this education is taken further, it is directed to special, lucrative matters; science is studied much the same way as one might choose a trade, learning no more about it than those applications which currently have well-known practical uses.

"In America, most of the rich people start off being poor; almost all those who do not work, were extremely busy in their youth. Therefore, when one could feel passion for study, there is no time to spend on it, and when one has time, there is no inclination to do so … . There are, then, a large number of people who have more or less the same notions on subjects such as religion, history, sciences, economic policies, law, government."

An extract from Volume I of *Democracy in America* by Alexis de Tocqueville, 1835.

potential force, the law-makers were becoming more representative of American democracy; the presidency of Andrew Jackson has traditionally been seen as especially important in this. The growing democratization of politics reflected other changes; the United States was not to be troubled by a proletariat of town dwellers driven off the land because in the West the possibility long existed of realizing the dream of independence; the social ideal of the independent smallholder could remain central to the American tradition. The opening up of the western hinterland by the Louisiana Purchase was as important in revolutionizing the wealth and population distributions which shaped American politics as was the commercial and industrial growth of the North.

THE WIDENING OF THE SLAVERY DEBATE

Above all, the opening of the West transformed the question of slavery. There was great scope for dispute about the terms on which new territories should be joined to the Union. As the organization first of the Louisiana Purchase and then territory taken from Mexico had to be settled, the inflammatory question was bound to be raised: was slavery to be permitted in the new territories? A fierce anti-slavery movement had arisen in the North which dragged the slavery issue to the forefront of American politics and kept it there until it overshadowed every other question. Its campaign for the ending of the slave trade and the eventual emancipation of the black slaves stemmed from much the same forces which had produced similar demands in other countries towards the end of the eighteenth century. But the American movement was importantly different, too. In the first place it was confronted with a *growth* of slavery at a time when it was disappearing elsewhere in the European world, so that the universal trend seemed to be at least checked, if not reversed, in the United States. Secondly, it involved a tangle of constitutional questions because of argument about the extent to which private property could be interfered with in individual states where local laws upheld it, or even in territories that were not yet states. Moreover the anti-slavery politicians brought forward a question which lay at the heart of the constitution, and, indeed, of the political life of every European country, too: who was to have the last word? The people were sovereign, that was clear:

but was the "people" the majority of its representatives in Congress, or the populations of individual states acting through their state legislatures and asserting the indefeasibility of their rights even against Congress? Thus slavery came by mid-century to be entangled with almost every question raised by American politics.

THE MISSOURI COMPROMISE

The great issues raised by slavery were just contained so long as the balance of power between the Southern and Northern states remained roughly the same. Although the North had a slight preponderance of numbers, the crucial equality in the Senate (where each state had two senators, regardless of its population or size) was maintained. Down to 1819, new states were admitted to the Union on an alternating system, one slave, one free; there were then eleven of each. Then came the first crisis, over the admission of the state of Missouri. In the days before the Louisiana Purchase French and Spanish law permitted slavery there and its settlers expected this to continue. They were indignant, and so were representatives of the Southern states, when a Northern congressman proposed restrictions upon slavery in the new state's constitution. There was great public stir and debate about sectional advantage; there was even talk of secession from the Union, so strongly did some Southerners feel. Yet the moral issue was muted. It was still possible to reach a political answer to a political question by the "Missouri Compromise" which admitted Missouri as a slave state, but balanced her by admitting Maine at the same time, and prohibiting any further extension of slavery in United States territory north of a line of latitude 36° 30'. This confirmed the doctrine that Congress had the right to keep slavery out of new territories if it chose to exercise it, but there was no reason to believe that the question would again arise for a long time. Indeed, so it proved until a generation had

Black slaves, such as those depicted here unloading provisions from a Mississippi steamship, constituted around one third of the South's population and made up the labour force on the plantations. In the mid-19th century, 80 per cent of the white population in the South had no slaves and only around 3,000 planters owned more than 100 slaves. In spite of this, the South almost unanimously asserted its right to retain slavery.

The United States and the slavery issue

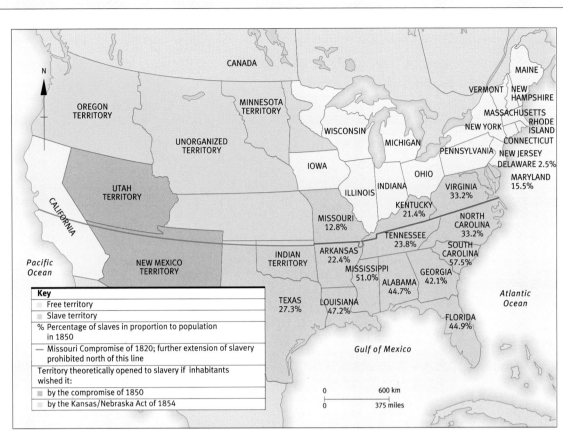

In 1815, those living south of the line that separated Maryland from Pennsylvania comprised half of the total population of the United States, and the South was expanding rapidly. Kentucky had become a state in 1792, Tennessee in 1796, Mississippi, Alabama and Missouri in 1821, Arkansas in 1836 and Florida and Texas in 1845. In the west and the north, nine new states had come from the Louisiana Purchase. Moreover, increasing numbers of immigrants were settling in the free states in the North. This meant that the Missouri Compromise of 1820, which banned slavery north of parallel 36° 30', and guaranteed a North–South balance, had become obsolete. In 1850, the political balance broke down. When the discovery of gold in California unleashed the gold rush, California applied for admission as a free state without having first been recognized as a territory, and was admitted into the Union. Although the interests of the North weighed heavily in Congress, the Senate was more evenly balanced between North and South, until 1859, when the incorporation of Kansas tipped the scales in favour of the North and the abolitionists.

passed. But already some had seen the future it contained: Thomas Jefferson, a former president and the man who drafted the Declaration of Independence, wrote that he "considered it at once as the knell of the Union", and another (future) president wrote in his diary that the Missouri question was "a mere preamble – a title-page to a great, tragic volume".

THE ABOLITIONIST CAMPAIGN

The tragedy did not come to a head for forty years. In part this was because Americans had much else to think about – territorial expansion above all – and in part because no question arose of incorporating territories suitable for cotton-growing, and therefore

Pro-abolitionist, Harriet Beecher-Stowe's book *Uncle Tom's Cabin*, published in 1852, had enormous impact on public opinion. This illustration from the original edition of the book shows a slave-owner attacking the book's hero.

requiring slave labour, until the 1840s. But there were soon forces at work to agitate public opinion and they would be effective when the public was ready to listen. It was in 1831 that a newspaper was established in Boston to advocate the unconditional emancipation of black slaves. This was the beginning of the "abolitionist" campaign of increasingly embittered propaganda, electoral pressure upon politicians in the North, assistance to runaway slaves and opposition to their return

to their owners after recapture, even when the law courts said they must be sent back. Against the background abolitionists provided, a struggle raged in the 1840s over the terms on which territory won from Mexico should be admitted. It ended in 1850 in a new Compromise, but one not to last long. From this time, politics were strained by increasing feelings of persecution and victimization among the Southern leaders and a growing arrogance on their part in the defence of their states' way of life. National party allegiances were already affected by the slavery issue; the Democrats took their stand on the finality of the 1850 settlement.

DESCENT TO DISASTER

The 1850s brought the descent to disaster. The need to organize Kansas blew up the truce which rested on the 1850 Compromise and brought about the first bloodshed as abolitionists strove to bully pro-slavery Kansas into accepting their views. There emerged a Republican party in protest against the proposal that the people living in the territory should decide whether Kansas should be slave or free: Kansas was north of the 36° 30' line. The anger of abolitionists now mounted, too, whenever the law supported the slave-owner, as it did in a notable Supreme Court decision in 1857 (in the "Dred Scott" case) which returned a slave to his master. In the South, on the other hand, such outcries were seen as incitements to disaffection among the blacks and a determination to use the electoral system against Southern liberties – a view which was, of course, justified, because the abolitionists, at least, were not men who would compromise, though they could not get the Republican party to support them. The Republican presidential candidate in the election of 1860 campaigned on a programme which, in so far as it concerned slavery, envisaged the exclusion of slavery only from territories to be brought into the Union in the future.

THE AMERICAN CIVIL WAR

THE 1860 CAMPAIGN PLATFORM was already too much for some Southerners. Although the Democrats were divided, the country voted on strictly sectional grounds in 1860; the Republican candidate Abraham Lincoln, who was to prove the greatest of American presidents, was elected by Northern states, together with the two Pacific coast ones. This was the end of the line for many Southerners. South Carolina formally seceded from the Union as a protest against the election. In February 1861 she was joined by six other states, and the Confederate States of America which they set up had its provisional government and president installed a month before President Lincoln was inaugurated in Washington.

Each side accused the other of revolutionary designs and behaviour. It is very difficult not to agree with both of them. The heart of the Northern position, as Lincoln saw, was that democracy should prevail, a claim assuredly of potentially limitless revolutionary implication. In the end, what the North achieved was indeed a social revolution in the South. On the other side, what the South was asserting in 1861 (and three more states joined the Confederacy after the first shots were fired) was that it had the same right to organize its life as had, say, revolutionary Poles or Italians in Europe. It is unfortunate, but generally true, that the coincidence of nationalist claims with liberal institutions is rarely exact, or even close, and never complete, but the defence of slavery was also a defence of self-determination. At the same time, though such great issues of principle were certainly at stake, they presented themselves in concrete, personal and local terms which make it very difficult to state clearly

Two runaway slaves about to be returned to slavery are marched through the streets of Boston to a steamer bound for South Carolina, whence they had fled. Some of the watching abolitionists weep as the manacled slaves are led past.

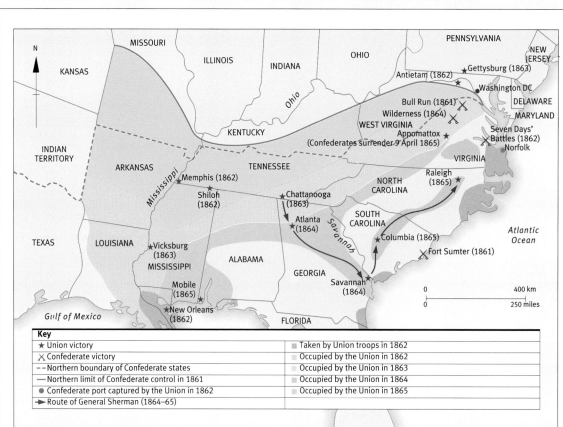

The American Civil War of 1861–1865 and dates of states' admission to the Union

In 1860 Abraham Lincoln, candidate for the Republican Party which had been established a few years earlier, was elected president. His electoral platform had included promises to increase tariffs and to prevent slavery from being introduced into the new western states. In February 1861, seven of the slave states agreed on secession and set up the Confederate States of America. When the federal government took steps to reinforce its garrisons in the South, the Southerners' attack on Fort Sumter started the Civil War. At first, the Confederates appeared to have the upper hand in the war, but as the fighting dragged on, the North's industrial and demographic superiority came to the fore.

the actual lines along which the republic divided for the great crisis of its history and identity. They ran through families, towns and villages, religions, and sometimes ran round groups of different colours. It is the tragedy of civil wars to be like that.

LINCOLN'S CHANGING AIMS

Once under way, war has a revolutionary potential of its own. Much of the particular impact of what one side called "the Rebellion" and the other side "the War between the States" grew out of the necessities of the struggle. It took four years for the Union forces to beat the Confederacy and in that time an important change had occurred in Lincoln's aims. At the beginning of the war he had spoken only of restoring the proper order of affairs: there were things happening in the Southern states, he told the people, "too powerful to be suppressed by the ordinary course of judicial proceedings" and they would require military operations. This view broadened into a consistent reiteration that the war was fundamentally about preserving the Union; Lincoln's aim in fighting was to reunite the states which composed it. For a long time this meant that he failed to satisfy those who sought from the war the abolition of slavery. But in the end he came round to it. In 1862 he could still say in a public letter that:

"If I could save the Union without freeing any slave, I would do it; and if I could save it by freeing all the slaves I would do it; and if I could save it by freeing some and leaving others alone, I would also do that,"

but he did so at a moment when he had already decided that he must proclaim the emancipation of slaves in the rebel states. It

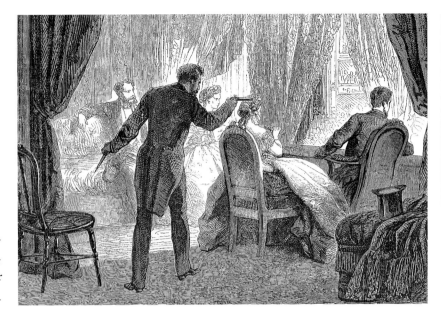

became effective on New Year's Day 1863; thus the nightmare of Southern politicians was reality at last, though only because of the war they had courted. It transformed the

President Lincoln is assassinated by a Southern fanatic, John Wilks Booth, at Ford's Theater in Washington.

Unionist soldiers pose with one of their guns during the Petersburg campaign against Confederates in Virginia, which lasted from June 1864 until April 1865.

nature of the struggle, though not very obviously. In 1865 the final step was taken in an amendment to the constitution which prohibited slavery anywhere in the United States. By that time the Confederacy was defeated, Lincoln had been murdered and the cause which he had imperishably summed up as "government of the people, by the people, for the people" was safe.

THE IMPLICATIONS OF THE NORTHERN VICTORY

In the aftermath of its military victory Lincoln's cause could hardly appear as an unequivocally noble or righteous one to all Americans, but its triumph was pregnant with importance not only for America but for all humanity. It was the only political event of the century whose implications were as far-reaching as, say, the Industrial Revolution. The war settled the future of the continent; one great power would continue to dominate the Americas and exploit the resources of the richest untapped domain yet known to be open to settlement. That fact in due course settled the outcome of two world wars and therefore the history of the world. The Union armies also decided that the system which would prevail in American politics would be the democratic one; this was not, perhaps, always true in the sense of Lincoln's words but the political institutions which in principle provided for the rule of the majority were henceforth secure from direct challenge. This was to have the incidental effect of linking democracy and material well-being closely in the minds of Americans; industrial capitalism in the United States would have a great pool of ideological commitment to draw upon when it faced its later critics.

THE SOCIAL CONSEQUENCES OF EMANCIPATION

There were other domestic consequences of emancipation, too. The most obvious was the creation of a new colour problem. In a sense there had been no colour problem while slavery existed. Servile status was the barrier separating the overwhelming majority of blacks (there had always been a few free among them) from whites, and it was upheld by legal sanctions. Emancipation swept away the framework of legal inferiority and replaced this with the framework, or myth, of democratic equality when very few Americans were ready to give this social reality. Millions of blacks in the South were suddenly free. They were also for the most part uneducated, largely untrained except for field labour, and virtually without leadership of their own race. For a little while in the Southern states they leant for support on the occupying armies of the Union; when this prop was removed blacks disappeared from the legislatures and public offices of the Southern states to which they had briefly aspired. In some areas they disappeared from the polling-booths, too. Legal disabilities were replaced by a social and physical coercion which was sometimes harsher than had been the old régime of slavery. Slaves at least had the value to their master of being an investment of capital; they were protected like other property and were usually ensured a minimum security and maintenance. Competition in a free labour market at a moment when the economy of large areas of the South was in ruins, with impoverished whites struggling for subsistence, was disastrous for the blacks. By the end of the century they had

Emancipation did not guarantee freed slaves access to American justice. In this engraving, dated 1911, a white Southern mob lynches an ex-slave accused of murdering a white woman.

been driven by a poor white population bitterly resentful of defeat and emancipation into social subordination and economic deprivation. From this was to stem emigration to the North in the twentieth century and racial problems in our own day.

THE TWO-PARTY SYSTEM

As another consequence of the war the United States retained a two-party system. Between them, Republicans and Democrats have continued to divide the presidency to this day, though sometimes threatened by third parties. There was nothing to make this probable before 1861. Many parties had come and gone, reflecting different movements in American society. But the war was to rivet upon the Democratic party a commitment to the Southern cause which at first was a grave handicap because it carried the stigma of disloyalty (no Democrat was president until 1885). Correspondingly, it won for the Republicans the loyalty of Northern states and the hopes of radicals who saw in them the saviours of the Union and democracy, and the liberators of the slave. Before the inadequacy of these stereotypes was clear, the parties were so deeply rooted in certain states that their predominance in them, let alone survival, was unchallengeable. Twentieth-century American politics would proceed by internal transformation of the two great parties which long reflected their primitive origins.

For the moment the Republicans of 1865 had it all their own way. Perhaps they would have found a way to reconcile the South if Lincoln had lived. As it was, the impact of their policies upon a defeated and devastated South made the "Reconstruction" years bitter ones. Many Republicans strove honestly to use the power they had to ensure democratic rights for the blacks; thus they ensured the future hegemony in the South of the Democrats. But they did not do too badly. Soon, too, the economic tide was with them as the great expansion interrupted briefly by the war was resumed.

A GROWING ECONOMY

American expansion had been going on for seventy years and was already prodigious. Its most striking manifestation had been territorial; it was about to become economic. The phase of America's advance to the point at which her citizens would have the highest per capita income in the world was just opening in the 1870s. In the euphoria of this huge blossoming of confidence and expectation, all political problems seemed for a while to have been solved. Under Republican administrations America turned, not for the last time, to the assurance that the business of America was not political debate but economic advance. The South remained largely untouched by the new prosperity and slipped even further behind the North; it had no political leverage until an issue capable of bringing support to the Democrats in other sections turned up.

The winning of the Far West

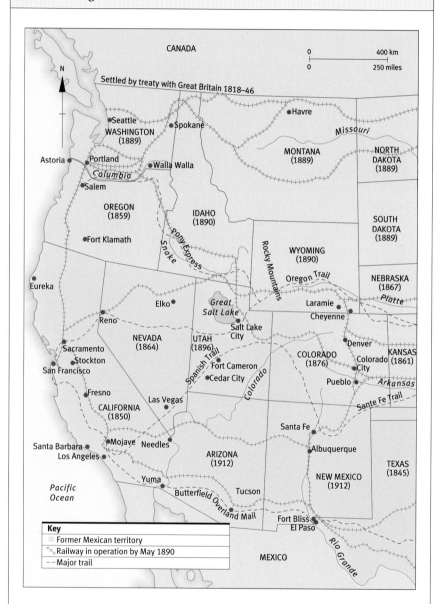

Key
- Former Mexican territory
- Railway in operation by May 1890
- Major trail

The development of the North American economy in the last 30 years of the 19th century was spectacular. For vast numbers of Europeans who lived in poverty the United States became, more than ever, the promised land. Transcontinental railways reinforced the national unity that had been won on the battlefields. In 1869 the first coast-to-coast rail link was completed and by 1900 there were three more, making the settlement of the West much easier. It also signalled the end of the North American Indians' way of life – they fought their final, desperate battles in these years.

THE MAGNETISM OF THE UNITED STATES

Meanwhile, the North and West could look back with confidence that the astonishing changes of the previous seventy years promised even better times ahead. Foreigners could feel this, too; that is why they were coming to the United States in growing numbers – two and a half million in the 1850s alone. They fed a population which had grown from just over five and a quarter million in 1800 to nearly forty million in 1870. About half of them by then lived west of the Alleghenies and the vast majority of them in rural areas. The building of railroads was opening the Great Plains to settlement and exploitation which had not yet really begun. In 1869 the golden spike was driven which marked the completion of the first transcontinental railroad link. In the new West the United States would find its greatest agricultural expansion; already, thanks to the shortage of labour experienced in the war years, machines were being used in numbers which pointed to a quite new scale of farming, the way to a new phase of the world's agricultural revolution which would make North America the granary of Europe. There were a quarter of a million mechanical reapers alone at work by the end of the war. Industrially, too, great years lay ahead; the United States was not yet an industrial power to compare with Great Britain (in 1870 there were still fewer than two million Americans employed in manufacturing), but the groundwork was done. With a large, increasingly well-off domestic market the prospects for American industry were bright.

Poised on the brink of their most confident and successful era, Americans were not being hypocritical in forgetting the losers. They understandably found it easy to do so in the general sense that the American system worked well. The blacks and the poor whites of the South had now joined the Native North Americans, who had been losers steadily for two centuries and a half, as the forgotten failures. The new poor of the growing Northern cities should probably not be regarded, comparatively, as losers; they were

A Union Pacific Railroad poster from 1869 advertises the opening of the USA's first transcontinental railroad. "Now is the time to seek your Fortune…" proclaims the poster, which also promotes the "luxurious cars and eating houses" the railroad has to offer.

The "Peterloo Massacre", pictured in this 19th-century painting, took place in Manchester, England, in 1819 when local magistrates sent the yeomanry (cavalry force) to St Peter's Fields to control a peaceful public meeting of supporters of political reform. Eleven people were killed and hundreds were injured in the ensuing panic. In the aftermath of the event, the Whigs called for parliamentary reform.

at least as well off, and probably better, than the poor of Manchester or Naples. Their willingness to come to the United States showed that she was already a magnet of great power. Nor was that power only material. Besides the "wretched refuse", there were the "huddled masses yearning to breathe free". The United States was in 1870 still a political inspiration to political radicals elsewhere, though perhaps her political practice and forms had more impact in Great Britain – where people linked (both approvingly and disapprovingly) democracy with the "Americanization" of British politics – than in continental Europe.

DEMOCRATIZING BRITISH POLITICS

Various transatlantic influences and connexions were aspects of the curious, fitful, but tenacious relations between the two Anglo-Saxon countries. They both underwent similar revolutionary change and here, perhaps, the achievement of Great Britain in the early nineteenth century is even more remarkable than the transformation of the

United States. At a time of unprecedented and potentially dislocating social upheaval, which turned her within a single lifetime into the first industrialized and urbanized society of modern times, Great Britain managed to maintain an astonishing constitutional and political continuity. At the same time, too, she was acting as a world and European power as the United States never had to, and ruled a great empire. In this setting she began the democratization of her institutions while retaining most of her buttresses of individual liberty.

Socially the United Kingdom was far less democratic than the United States in 1870 (if the blacks are set aside as a special case). Social hierarchy (conferred by birth and land if possible, but if not, money would sometimes do) stratified the United Kingdom; every observer was struck by the assured confidence of the English ruling classes that they were meant to rule. There was no American West to offset the deep swell of deference with the breeze of frontier democracy; Canada and Australia attracted restless emigrants, but in so doing removed the possibility of their changing the tone of English society. Political democracy developed faster than social, on the other hand, even if the universal male suffrage already long-established in the United States would not be introduced until 1918; the democratization of English politics was already past the point of reversibility by 1870.

THE ENLARGEMENT OF THE ELECTORATE

The democratization of English politics had come about within a few decades. Though it had deeply libertarian institutions – equality at law, effective personal liberty, a representative system – the English constitution of 1800 had not rested on democratic principles. Its basis was the representation of certain individual and historic rights and the sovereignty of the Crown in Parliament. The accidents of the past produced from these elements an electorate large by contemporary European standards, but as late as 1832, the word "democratic" was a pejorative one and few thought it indicated a desirable goal. To most English people, democracy meant the French Revolution and military despotism. Yet the most important step towards democracy in the English political history of the century was taken in 1832. This was the passing of a Reform Act which was not itself democratic and was, indeed, intended by many of those who supported it to act as a barrier to democracy. It carried out a great revision of the representative system, removing anomalies (such as the tiny constituencies which had been effectively controlled by patrons), to provide parliamentary constituencies which

better (though still far from perfectly) reflected the needs of a country of growing industrial cities, and above all to change and make more orderly the franchise. It had been based on a jumble of different principles in different places; now, the main categories of persons given the vote were freeholders in the rural areas, and householders who owned or paid rent for their house at a middle-class level in the towns. The model elector was the man with a stake in the country, although dispute about the precise terms of the franchise still left some oddities. The immediate result was an electorate of about 650,000 and a House of Commons which did not look very different from its predecessor. None the less, dominated by the aristocracy as it still was, it marked the beginning of nearly a century during which British politics were to be completely democratized, because once the constitution had been changed in this way, then it could be changed again and the House

This contemporary satire is entitled *The Reformers' Attack on the Old Rotten Tree*. The Reform Act of 1832, which, as well as extending the franchise, eliminated many of the "Rotten Boroughs", is widely thought to have prevented the threat of a British revolution from being realized.

of Commons more and more claimed the right to say what should be done. In 1867, another Act produced an electorate of about two million and in 1872 the decision that voting should take place by secret ballot followed: a great step.

PEEL AND CONSERVATISM

The process of democratizing English politics would not be completed before the twentieth century, but it soon brought other changes in the nature of British politics. Slowly, and somewhat grudgingly, the traditional political class began to take account of the need to organize parties which were something more than family connexions or personal cliques of Members of Parliament. This was much more obvious after the emergence of a really big electorate in 1867. But the implication – that

there was a public opinion to be courted which was more than that of the old landed class – was grasped sooner than this. All the greatest of English parliamentary leaders in the nineteenth century were men whose success rested on their ability to catch not only the ear of the House of Commons, but that of important sections of society outside it. The first and possibly most significant example was Sir Robert Peel, who created English Conservatism. By accepting the verdicts of public opinion he gave Conservatism a pliability which always saved it from the intransigence into which the right was tempted in so many European countries.

The great political crisis of Corn Law Repeal demonstrated this. It was not only about economic policy; it was also about who should govern the country, and was in some ways a complementary struggle to that for parliamentary reform before 1832. By the

A Summer's Day in Hyde Park was painted by John Ritchie in 1858. A new degree of middle-class wealth was one sign of mid-Victorian social changes.

middle of the 1830s the Conservatives had been brought by Peel to accept the consequences of 1832, and in 1846 he was just able to make them do the same over the protective Corn Laws, whose disappearance showed that landed society no longer had the last word. Vengefully, his party, the stronghold of the country gentlemen who considered the agricultural interests the embodiment of England and themselves the champions of the agricultural interest, turned on Peel soon afterwards and rejected him. They were right in sensing that the whole tendency of his policy had been directed to the triumph of the free trade principles which they associated with the middle-class manufacturers. Their decision divided their party and condemned it to paralysis for twenty years, but Peel had in fact rid them of an incubus. He left it free when reunited to compete for the electorate's goodwill untrammelled by commitment to the defence of only one among several economic interests.

VICTORIAN ACHIEVEMENTS

The redirection of British tariff and fiscal policies towards free trade was one side, though in some ways the most spectacular, of a general alignment of British politics towards reform and liberalization in the central third of the century. During this time a beginning was made with local government reform (significantly, in the towns, not in the countryside where the landed interest was still the master), a new Poor Law was introduced, factory and mining legislation was passed and began to be effectively policed by inspection, the judicial system was reconstructed, disabilities on protestant nonconformists, Roman Catholics and Jews were removed, the ecclesiastical monopoly of matrimonial law which went back to Anglo-Saxon times was ended, a

postal system was set up which became the model on which other nations would shape theirs, and a beginning was even made with tackling the scandalous neglect of public education. All this was accompanied by unprecedented growth in wealth, whose confident symbol was the holding in 1851 of a Great Exhibition of the world's wares in London under the patronage of the queen herself and the direction of her consort. If the British were inclined to bumptiousness, as they seem to have been in the central decades of Victoria's reign, then it may be said that they had grounds. Their institutions and economy had never looked healthier.

Dated 1858, this view of the interior of the House of Commons, inside London's new Houses of Parliament, was painted by Joseph Nash (1802–1878).

Governments and the middle classes loved progress and showed it. The Crystal Palace in London, pictured in this contemporary illustration, was the venue for the Great Exhibition, the first of its kind in the world, which opened on 1 May, 1851.

Not that everyone was pleased. Some moaned about a loss of economic privilege: in fact, the United Kingdom continued to display extremes of wealth and poverty as great as any other country's. There was somewhat more substance to the fear of creeping centralization. Parliamentary legislative sovereignty led to bureaucracy invading more and more areas which had previously been immune to government intervention in practice. England in the nineteenth century was very far from concentrating power in her state apparatus to the degree which has now become usual in all countries. Yet some people felt worried that she might be going the way of France, a country whose highly centralized administration was taken to be sufficient explanation of the failure to achieve liberty which had accompanied the French success in establishing equality. In offsetting such a tendency, the Victorian reforms of local government, some of which came only in the last two decades of the century, were crucial.

AVOIDING REVOLUTION

Some foreigners admired the British political system. Most wondered how, in spite of the appalling conditions of her factory towns, the United Kingdom had somehow navigated the rapids of popular unrest which had proved fatal to orderly government in other states. She had deliberately undertaken huge reconstructions of her institutions at a time when the dangers of revolution were clearly apparent elsewhere, and had emerged unscathed, her power and wealth enhanced and the principles of liberalism even more apparent in her politics. Her statesmen and historians gloried in reiterating that the essence of the nation's life was freedom, in a famous phrase, "broadening down from precedent to

precedent". The English seemed fervently to believe this, yet it did not lead to license. The country did not have the advantages of geographical remoteness and almost limitless land which were enjoyed by the United States – and even the United States had fought one of the bloodiest wars in human history to contain a revolution. How, then, had Great Britain done it?

This was a leading question, though one historians still sometimes ask without thinking about its implications: that there exist certain conditions which make revolution likely and that British society seems to have fulfilled them. It may be, rather, that no such propositions need to be conceded. Perhaps there never was a potentially revolutionary threat in this rapidly changing society. Many of the basic changes which the French Revolution brought to Europe had already existed in Great Britain for centuries, after all. The fundamental institutions, however rusty or encrusted with inconvenient historic accretion they might be, offered large possibilities. Even in unreformed days, the House of Commons and House of Lords were not the closed corporate institutions which were all that was available in many European states. Already before 1832, they had shown their capacity to meet new needs, even if slowly and belatedly; the first Factory Act (not, admittedly, a very effective one) had been passed as early as 1801. Once 1832 was past, then there were good grounds for thinking that if Parliament were only pressed hard enough from the outside, it would carry out any reforms that were required. There was no legal restraint on its power to do so. Even the oppressed and angry seem to have seen this. There were many outbreaks of desperate violence and many revolutionaries about in the 1830s and 1840s (which were especially hard times for the poor) but it is striking that the most important popular movement of the

Queen Victoria, whose coronation is pictured here, reigned from 1837 to her death in 1901. Her long rule became the symbol of an era of British progress, certainty, conquest and wealth.

day, the great spectrum of protest gathered together in what was called "Chartism", asked in the People's Charter which was its programme for measures which would make Parliament more responsive to popular needs, not for its abolition.

TRADITIONAL PATTERNS OF BEHAVIOUR

It is not likely that Parliament would have been called upon to provide reform unless other factors had operated. Here it is perhaps significant that the great reforms of Victorian England were all ones which interested the middle classes as much as the masses, with the possible exception of factory legislation. The English middle class came to an early share in political power as its continental counterparts had not and could therefore use it to obtain change; it was not tempted to ally with revolution, the recourse of desperate individuals to whom other avenues were closed. But in any case it does not seem that the English masses were themselves very revolutionary. At any rate, their failure to act in a revolutionary way has caused much distress

to later left-wing historians. Whether this is because their sufferings were too great, not great enough or whether simply there were too many differences between different sections of the working class has been much disputed. But it is at least worth noticing, as did contemporary visitors, that in England traditional patterns of behaviour died hard; it was long to remain a country with habits of deference to social superiors which much struck foreigners – especially Americans. Moreover, there were working-class organizations which provided alternatives to revolution. They were often "Victorian" in their admirable emphasis on self-help, caution, prudence, sobriety. Of the elements making up the great English Labour movement, only the political party which bears that name was not in existence already before 1840; the others were mature by the 1860s. The "friendly societies" for insurance against misfortune, the cooperative associations and, above all, the trades unions all provided effective channels for personal participation in the improvement of working-class life, even if at first only to a few and slowly. This early maturity was to underlie the paradox of English socialism, its later dependence on a very conservative and unrevolutionary trade-union movement, long the largest in the world.

Once the 1840s were over, economic trends may have helped to allay discontent. At any rate working-class leaders often said so, almost regretfully; they, at least, thought that betterment told against a revolutionary danger in England. As the international economy picked up in the 1850s good times came to the industrial cities of a country which was the workshop of the world and its merchant, banker, and insurer, too. As employment and wages rose, the support which the Chartists had mustered crumbled away and they were soon only a reminiscence.

A DOMESTICATED MONARCHY

The symbols of the unchanging form which contained so much change were the central institutions of the kingdom: Parliament and the Crown. When the Palace of Westminster was burned down and a new one was built, a mock-medieval design was chosen to emphasize the antiquity of the Mother of Parliaments. The violent changes of the most revolutionary era of British history thus continued to be masked by the robes of custom and tradition. Above all, the monarchy continued. Already when Victoria ascended the throne, it was second only to the papacy in antiquity among the political institutions of Europe; yet it was much changed in reality, for all that. It had been brought very low in public esteem by George III's successor, the worst of English kings, and not much enhanced by his heir. Victoria and her husband were to make it again unquestioned. In part this was against the grain for the queen herself; she did not pretend to like the political neutrality appropriate to a constitutional monarch when the Crown had withdrawn above the political battle. None the less, it was in her reign that this withdrawal was seen to be made. She also domesticated the monarchy; for the first time since the days of the young George III the phrase "the Royal Family" was a reality and could be seen to be such. It was one of many ways in which her German husband, Prince Albert, helped her, though he got little thanks for it from an ungrateful English public.

THE IRISH FAILURE

Only in Ireland did their capacity for imaginative change seem always to fail the British people. They had faced a real revolutionary danger and had had to put down a rebellion there in 1798. In the 1850s and 1860s things were quiet. But the reason was in large measure an appalling disaster which overtook Ireland in the middle of the 1840s when the failure of the potato crop was followed by famine, disease and thus, brutally, a Malthusian solution to Ireland's over-population. For the moment, the demand for the repeal of the Act of Union which had joined her to Great Britain in 1801 was muted, the dislike of her predominantly Catholic population for an alien and established Protestant Church was in abeyance and there was no serious disturbance among a peasant population feeling no loyalty to absentee English landlords. Problems none the less remained and the Liberal government

Anti-British demonstrations took place in Dublin's Phoenix Park during the unrest that followed the suspension of habeas corpus in 1882. In the face of the arrest of anti-British activists in Ireland, two British ministers were assassinated in Dublin.

which took office in 1868 addressed itself above all else to them. All that emerged was a new Irish nationalism movement, demanding "Home Rule". This demand was to haunt British politics and overturn their combinations and settlements for the rest of the century and beyond. Through the capacity Home Rule was to show to wreck British Liberalism, Ireland again became a force in world history after over a thousand years. She was also to make another important, if less direct, impact upon it at about the same time, through the Irish emigration to the United States.

Evicted tenants in County Kerry, Ireland, watch while their homes are burned. During the Irish Land War of 1879–1881, tenant farmers struggled against rising rents and evictions following an agricultural depression and eventually persuaded the British prime minister, William Gladstone, to meet their demands, in the Irish Land Act of 1881.

Mirror telescope

The mirror telescope, which was first constructed by Isaac Newton in 1671 and later perfected by William Herschel, produced large images that allowed the user to study distant heavenly bodies.

1714
Peace of Utrecht

Savoy is granted Sardinia
in exchange for Sicily

1710

1720

The spinning-jenny, a machine that spun and wound yarn on to spindles, was invented by James Hargreaves in 1764. It was to revolutionize the British cotton and wool industries.

A spinning-jenny

1750

1760

1756–1763
The Seven Years' War

The prominent *sans-culotte* Pierre Chaumette (1763–1794) is shown unveiling the Altar to Reason in Notre Dame, Paris, in November 1793. The French king, Louis XVI, was executed in the same year.

Altar to Reason

Napoleon crossing the Alps is portrayed by David in 1801. Napoleon's dictatorship, as First Consul and later as Emperor of France, lasted until 1814.

Napoleon Bonaparte

1787
Constitution of the
United States

1789
Start of French
Revolution

1798
Napoleon's
campaign in Egypt

1790

1800

1788
First British convicts
sent to Australia

1792
French Republic
is declared

1795
The Directory
in France

1799
The Consulate
in France

1801
The Act of Union joins
Ireland to Great Britain

1804
Napoleon
becomes Emper

1832
Parliamentary
reform in Britain

1837
Victoria becomes Queen
of Britain and Ireland

1830

1840

1825
December uprising
in St Petersburg

1845–1851
Great Famine
in Ireland

Liberty Leading the People, painted by Eugène Delacroix (1798–1863), is a heroic portrayal of the French July Revolution of 1830, during which the people of Paris rose against Charles X. A new king, Louis Philippe, was installed on the throne.

July Revolution in France

The German socialist Karl Marx, who wrote *The Communist Manifesto*, died in 1883. His theory of historical inevitability profoundly influenced the international socialist movement.

Karl Marx

1867
Creation of Austro-
Hungarian Empire

Franco-Prussian War

1870

1880

1866
Austro-
Prussian War

1871
The Paris Commune
Prussian Second Reich

1878
Independence of Romania,
Serbia and Montenegro

Isaac Newton

In his *Principia*, which was published in 1687, Isaac Newton (1642–1727) demonstrated how gravity sustains the physical universe.

1740–1748
Austrian War of
Succession

1730   1740

The first armed conflict of the American War of Independence (1775–1783) took place on 18 April 1775. Here, Britain's General Burgoyne is shown surrendering to the American leader General Gates at Saratoga Springs in 1777.

American War of Independence

1768
Cook's first voyage

1771
Arkwright's first
water frame

1774
The Philadelphia
Congress

1783
Great Britain recognizes
independent United States

1770   1780

1772
The first division
of Poland

1773
The Boston
Tea Party

1776
American Declaration of
Independence

1806
Confederation of
the Rhine is formed

1809
First steam ship

1811–1812
Luddite movement
in England

1814–1824
Reign of Louis
XVIII of France

1819
Customs Union of
Germanic states set up

1823
Monroe
doctrine

1810   1820

1805
Battle of
Trafalgar

1807
Creation of the Grand
Duchy of Warsaw

1812
Napoleon's
campaign in Russia

1815
Battle of Waterloo and
the Treaty of Vienna

1821–1828
War of Independence
in Greece

A new revolutionary wave swept across Europe in 1848 – a period labelled the "springtime of the nations" by liberals. For a while, the unrest seemed to threaten the peace settlement of 1815.

Rioting in Poland in 1848

1853–1856
The Crimean War

1859
Beginning of the
unification of Italy

1863
Polish uprising

1850   1860

1846
Repeal of the Corn Laws
in Great Britain

1851
Great Exhibition
in London

1852
Second Empire
in France

1855–1881
Reign of Russian
Tsar Alexander II

1861–1865
The American
Civil War

1864
First Socialist
International

1889
Second Socialist
International

1894
Franco-Russian
Alliance

1901
Death of Victoria, Queen of Britain
and Ireland and Empress of India

1890   1900

1888
William II becomes
German Emperor

1899–1902
The Boer War

VOLUME 7 *Chapters and contents*

Chapter 4

Political change: a new Europe 114

Chapter 5

Political change: the Anglo-Saxon world 150

SERIES CONTENTS

INDEX

Page references to main text in roman, to box text in **bold** and to captions in *italic*.

ACKNOWLEDGMENTS

The publishers wish to thank the following for their kind permission to reproduce the illustrations in this book:

KEY

b bottom; **c** centre; **t** top; **l** left; **r** right
AISA: Archivo Iconográfico S.A., Barcelona
AKG: AKG, London
BAL: Bridgeman Art Library, London / New York
BM: British Museum, London
BN: Bibliothèque Nationale, Paris
DBP: Duncan Baird Publishers, London
ET: e.t. Archive, London
JLC: Jean-Loup Charmet, Paris
MEPL: Mary Evans Picture Library, London
MNCV: Musée National du Château de Versailles, Paris
NPG: National Portrait Gallery, London
NWPA: North Wind Picture Archives, Alfred, Maine
RMN: Réunion des Musées Nationaux, Paris

Front cover: BAL / Musée du Petit Palais, Paris
3 Christie's Images, London
7 Oronoz / Galleria dell'Accademia, Venice
8 Alinari-Giraudon
9t BAL / Rafael Valls Gallery, London
9b Museo del Prado, Madrid
10 BAL / Musée Condé, Chantilly
11 BAL / BM
12 Rijksmuseum, Amsterdam
13 AISA / Biblioteca Central de Cataluña, Barcelona
14 AISA / Biblioteca Central de Cataluña, Barcelona
15 BAL / Louvre, Paris
16 BAL / Christie's, London
17 Oronoz / Musei Vaticani, Vatican City
18 NPG
19t The Royal Society, London
19b Science & Society Picture Library / Science Museum, London
20 BN
21 ET / Tate Gallery, London
22t AISA
22b Muzeum Okregowew, Torunin
23 BAL / Biblioteca Marucelliana, Florence
24 NPG
25 BAL / Derby Museum & Art Gallery
26 AISA
27 AISA / Galleria degli Uffizi, Florence
28 BN
29 AKG / Erich Lessing / Musée des Beaux-Arts, Dijon
30 Musée Carnavalet, Paris / Habouzit
31 AKG / Erich Lessing / BN
33 AISA
34 AKG
35 Oronoz
36 AKG

37 Kunsthistorisches Museum, Vienna
38 Musée Carnavalet, Paris
39 BAL / Kunsthalle, Hamburg
41 Tate Gallery, London
42 Hulton Getty Collection, London
43 Index-BAL / NPG
44 BN
45 BN
47 BN
48 National Gallery, London
49 BN
50t Scala / Museo del Passagio, Pallanza
50b Museo del Prado, Madrid
51 RMN / Musée des Beaux-Arts, Nantes
53t RMN / R. G. Ojeda / Louvre, Paris
53b MEPL
54t Oronoz
54b MEPL
55 BAL / Royal Holloway & Bedford New College, Surrey
56t Lauros-Giraudon / Musée National des Techniques, Paris
56b AISA
57 Walker Art Gallery, Liverpool / Board of Trustees of the National Museums and Galleries on Merseyside
58 BAL / Institute of Civil Engineers, London
59 JLC
60 Courtesy of Sheffield Art Galleries and Museums
61 Novosti, London
62 Peter Newark's Historical Pictures
63 Bildarchiv Preussischer Kulturbesitz, Berlin
64 JLC
65 BM
66 BAL / Wallington Hall, Northumberland
67 BAL / Private Collection
68 MEPL
69 MEPL
71 JLC / Musée Carnavalet, Paris
72 NPG, London
73 NWPA
74 RMN / MNCV
75 © The Metropolitan Museum of Art, New York
76 BN
77 BN
78 AISA / Biblioteca Nacional, Madrid
79 Oronoz / Academia de Bellas Artes de San Fernando, Madrid
80 Peter Newark's Historical Pictures
81 BAL / Hall of Representatives, Washington D. C.
82 Peter Newark's Historical Pictures
83 Oronoz
84 NWPA
85 BAL / Private Collection
86 BAL / MNCV
87 RMN / MNCV
88 BN
89 JLC
90 RMN / MNCV
91 BN

92 BN
93t BN
93b Musée Carnavalet, Paris / Andreani
94 BAL / Musée Carnavalet, Paris
95l & r BN
96 Musée Carnavalet, Paris / Berthier
97 AKG / Erich Lessing / MNCV
98 AKG
99 ET / Musée Carnavalet, Paris
100 BAL / New College, Oxford University, Oxford
101 Musée Carnavalet, Paris / Andreani
102t BAL / State Hermitage Museum, St Petersburg
102b RMN / Gérard Blot / MNCV
103 RMN / Louvre, Paris
104 Oronoz / Musée National des Châteaux de Malmaison et de Bois-Préau, Rueil-Malmaison
105 Deutsches Historisches Museum, Berlin
106 BAL / Biblioteca Nazionale, Turin
108 AKG / Steiermärkisches Landesmuseum, Austria
109 Museo del Prado, Madrid
110 ET / Fondation Thiers, Paris
111 Oronoz
113 Christie's Images, London
114 BAL / Lauros-Giraudon / Louvre, Paris
115 NPG
117 BAL / Lauros-Giraudon / Musée Carnavalet, Paris
118 RMN / Louvre, Paris
119 BAL / Wolverhampton Art Gallery
120 ET / Musée Carnavalet, Paris
121 RMN / MNCV
122t RMN / A. Danvers / Musée des Beaux-Arts, Bordeaux
122b RMN / Hervé Lewandowski / Louvre, Paris
123 Heeresgeschichtliches Museum, Vienna
124 Index / Raccolte Bertarelli, Milan
125t Oronoz
125b Historisches Museum, Frankfurt-am-Main
126 AKG / Museum Ostdeutsche Galerie, Regensburg
127 ET
128 Novosti, London
129 BN
130 BAL / Lauros-Giraudon / MNCV
131 Scala / Museo del Risorgimento, Milan
132 Scala / Museo del Risorgimento, Rome
133 Index / JLC / Musée Carnavalet, Paris
135 JLC / Musée Carnavalet, Paris
136 BAL / Peter Willi Private Collection
137 Science & Society Picture Library / National Railway Museum, London
138t BN
138b Deutsches Historisches Museum, Berlin
140 ET / State Historical Museum, Moscow
141 Scala / State Tretyakov Gallery, Moscow
142 AISA / State Russian Museum, St Petersburg
144 AKG
145 AISA / State Tretyakov Gallery, Moscow
146t Index-BAL / State Tretyakov Gallery, Moscow

146b Giraudon / State Russian Museum, St Petersburg
147 AISA / State Tretyakov Gallery, Moscow
149 MEPL
150 Birmingham Museum & Art Gallery
151 AKG
152 ET
153 NWPA
154 BN
155t BAL / American Museum, Bath
155b BAL / Private Collection
157 Oronoz
158 BAL / Lauros-Giraudon
160 BN
162 DBP
163 NWPA
165t BN
165b AKG
166 MEPL
167 AISA
169 Peter Newark's Historical Pictures
170 Ardea London Ltd
171 ET
172 Museum of London
173 BAL / Houses of Parliament, Westminster, London
174 BAL / Victoria & Albert Museum, London
176 BAL / Bradford Art Galleries and Museums
177 Oronoz / BN
179 NWPA

MAPS
All maps copyright © 1998 Helicon/Debate

TEXT CREDITS
The publishers wish to thank the following for their kind permission to reproduce the translations and copyright material in this book. Every effort has been made to trace copyright owners, but if anyone has been omitted we apologize and will, if informed, make corrections in any future edition.

p.26 extract from *An Answer to the Question: 'What is Enlightenment?'* from *Political Writings* by Immanuel Kant, translated by H. B. Nisbet. Copyright © Cambridge University Press, 1970, 1991. Reproduced by permission of Cambridge University Press; p.27 extract from *Discourse on Method and the Meditations* by René Descartes, translated by F. E. Sutcliffe, 1968 (Penguin Classics 1968) copyright © F. E. Sutcliffe, 1968. Reproduced by permission of Penguin Books Ltd.; p.33 extract from *The Spirit of the Laws* by Montesquieu, translated and edited by Anne M. Cohler, Basia C. Miller and Harold S. Stone. Copyright © Cambridge University Press, 1989. Reproduced by permission of Cambridge University Press; p.143 extract from *The Bronze Horseman* from *Narrative Poems* by Alexander Pushkin and Michael Lermontov, translated by